The Technique of
Oil Painting

The
Technique of
Oil Painting

Colin Hayes

 REINHOLD PUBLISHING CORPORATION
NEW YORK

© Colin Hayes 1965

Published in the United States of America 1965
by Reinhold Publishing Corporation
Library of Congress Catalog Card Number : 65–26474

Published by Reinhold Publishing Corporation
430 Park Avenue, New York, N.Y.

Made and printed in Great Britain
by William Clowes and Sons, Limited
London and Beccles

Contents

What is painting?

The Impressionist painter Renoir was once persuaded to write the introduction to an edition of Cennino Cennini's famous treatise on painting, and he made it the opportunity to write a little essay on the subject of Technique. If the Greeks, Renoir said, had left a treatise on painting, it would be like Cennini's. Until the break-up of the old European tradition all artists painted in the same way because some common bond impelled them to do so. But now (Renoir was writing in 1910), this tradition is lost; everyone paints as he can. And this is as it must be; for the ancient tradition was held together by faith in religious subject-matter, a faith which crossed boundaries of time and place. He berated attempts to form Brotherhoods of artists in the medieval manner, for they ended not by glorifying cathedrals, but by decorating railway stations.

Now of course Renoir was exaggerating in a Shavian way, but he was making an essential point. With or without the compulsion of Inner Faith, painters who were led by the desire (indeed necessity) to depict the same subject-matter in the same way used much the same methods throughout centuries. There was an evolutionary process by which the Craft of Painting gradually acquired, and as gradually discarded, its techniques. Only the greatest masters who rose above their times were able to illuminate the hidden truth that technique must evolve from artistic vision, that new ways of putting on the paint must await new ways of looking at things.

But our era shows the reverse side of the coin, for it has been overwhelmingly concerned with things seen in new ways, and indeed with new things seen in new ways. Two hundred years ago students could leave the Academies with one method of working which might take them to the heights; one hundred years ago the young Impressionists were already emerging dissatisfied from the École des Beaux-Arts and the studio of Gleyre to seek salvation in the independent ideas of Courbet, Manet and Daubigny. Renoir himself, brought up from porcelain painting through the Beaux-Arts to association with Manet, Degas, Monet and Cézanne, had finally to find a way of painting like Renoir.

Perhaps the Impressionists were the first group of painters who fully made plain the new condition of the artist. The old artist, who sought employment as a painter, hoped to be better than his fellows; the moderns, who paint and seek to sell their wares, must also be different from them.

Here is the modern difficulty in writing a book about the technique of painting. The student who is led by one rigid course of instruction in the application of paint is not so much introduced to painting as to a certain kind of painting, and who is to know if this is what he will need? Of course there is a school of thought, subscribed to by critics and connoisseurs more than by artists, who think that painting can no longer be taught at all, and that every artist must find his own salvation from birth. But I think that this conception of the modern artist is basically a romantic one and that it is gradually losing ground. It certainly takes little account of the fact that although 'originality' may be the hunting-cry of the contemporary art world, the difference between the amateur painter and the professional painter is still as apparent and pronounced as ever. And professional painting is still one which displays in its creator not only experience but knowledge. How then can a teacher, let alone a book, help the student of painting?

There are purely technical aspects of painting still to be learnt; there are certain basic rules relevant to each medium which the painter ignores at his peril—or at his painting's physical peril. If he begins a work in oil and finishes it in glue he need not expect it to survive. On the other hand a long and blin-kered training in the old grisaille method of portrait painting will almost certainly be of as little use to him as it would have been to Van Gogh.

I think that the student can still be helped, but that he learns best nowadays if the technical and pictorial aspects of painting are allowed to proceed hand in hand. Paints and media have certain physical properties which make them act in certain ways, and the student must learn enough about these properties to keep himself out of difficulty. But the young artist can no longer start out by simply mastering the business of grinding pigments, of preparing oils and resins and laying grounds on canvas and panels, like the apprentices of the old masters. (Modern masters do not usually have apprentices and when they do they often avoid employing students. The student wants to learn too much about painting as an art and it is inevitable that he should.) So because painting is so much more of a diffuse activity these days, the processes of both learning and teaching are more oblique. I believe that nowadays a student can only approach painting technically by approaching it aesthetically. He must have some idea of what he is doing and why he is doing it, while he is discovering how to do it. It is not only that there is more than one way and one style of painting; it is that the young artist is very well aware of the fact. If he has the urge to start, his interest in painting can hardly have left him so innocent as not to know that a multiplicity of different styles and pictorial theories will await his attention; indeed more will have been invented by the time he has ceased to be a student.

But if the world is his oyster, he must still learn to distinguish pearls from paste. He is more than ever in danger of learning techniques whose origin and *raison d'être* he does not understand and this is the first stage of decline towards a manner of painting dependent on technical tricks. He still needs to learn that technical tricks are not the same thing as skill. Tricks, which can be learnt very easily and very quickly, come more and more to hide an emptiness which is the characteristic of debased art. Skill grows slowly (and often painfully) out of the need to clarify and strengthen a genuine artistic statement.

It is for such reasons that I am not starting this book with an exposition on the nature of pigments, nor on the methods of priming canvas. These things have their place. But I have seen more than enough of young students carried away by an enthusiasm for pestles and mortars, sun-dried oils and special grounds concocted from prized recipes.

Some who can talk for hours on such matters cannot talk for five minutes about the theories of Seurat or the colour of Matisse. It is enough for them that one was something to do with atmosphere and that the other is pleasantly decorative. It is not surprising when their own work displays a turgid technical cuisine with a corresponding emptiness of pictorial ideas.

Now of course if the student can get 'bogged down' in technique it is no less true that he can stifle his painting with aesthetic theories, and I do not wish to alarm the reader. I am not about to embark on a history of modern aesthetic theory, even were I qualified to do so. Still less do I wish to lead him through a series of chapters on how to paint in the Cubist manner, the Fauvist manner, the Abstract, the Impressionist manner or even a Realist manner. What I want to do is to introduce the reader to the 'technique' and practice of painting —that is to its materials and what may be done with them—by discussing first some at least of the things that painting can be about. I must make assumptions and will doubtless display prejudices and limitations.

The first assumption I must make is that the reader is among those students whose art takes its starting point in the observation of external reality, and who are excited enough by what they see to make some part of it the subject-matter of their paintings. My reasons for this are twofold. First, I know of no way of teaching the practice of specifically abstract or non-figurative painting which does not reduce itself either to the advocacy of one or more recognised styles or to recommending the employment of a selection of technical tricks. Secondly, I must admit that I am among those who remain unconvinced that non-figurative art can, as it were, grow out of itself. It seems to me that the pictorial expression of a particular visual experience has provided both the initial training and a continuing source of ideas for the best abstract art. Perhaps this is just another way of saying that the abstract artist who displays (or betrays) a figurative history is the kind I prefer. Both Mondrian with his formalism and Klee with his fantasy condense reality in a way which is true for me, whereas some other abstract or symbolic painters are as false and illusionist as any debased photographic Salon painter.

Representational painting today is probably freer to branch out in personal directions than it has ever been, and if the technique which an artist develops may to some extent arise out of any one of these directions, it is necessary to find some common ground on which to start thinking about the problems. This is perhaps not quite as difficult as it sounds. Although figurative painting can take many different forms, there are some forms it can no longer take and others which it ought not to take. It can no longer, for instance, look like Early Flemish painting. We do not really know how to do it, and if we did, we would deceive ourselves in supposing that we could either recapture its spirit, or ignore all that has gone after. We are on more objective ground when we try to define what painting is not; to put it another way, what 'non-painting' is. It is not necessarily the same thing as bad painting, although since the invention of the camera it has often been so. It seems to me, and this may be just opinion, that attempts to make a total imitation of the surface appearance of nature may lead to 'non-painting'. At any rate, I should make it clear that *trompe l'œil* painting, the attempt to provide the spectator with the illusion that he is looking at an actual flower or a real apple, is not the concern of this book.

Now ultimately of course, the style, quality and technique of a painting must belong to the individual artist. But I have said that art students do not come innocent into the world, artistically speaking; if I am to define the kinds of 'ready-made' starting points which figurative painting offers him, I would say that they are those which arise out of what the Impressionists made of the natural world, out of the later developments of Impressionism, and even out of the reactions against them. I do not mean that students must learn to paint like the Impressionists or their followers, but rather that the liberating effect of this great movement on our view of appearances has not really been superseded by any profoundly new form of visual freedom. Indeed since the 1950s many *avant-garde* painters have leant more towards the characteristic marks of Impressionism than did their immediate predecessors.

But while figurative painting has taken on a quite fresh look over the past century, has discovered new things to look at, and new ways of painting them, it has not discarded all the traditional attributes but rather put them to its own uses. A student should clearly understand what at least some of these attributes are, so that he may equip himself with the basic vocabulary of painting. When Cézanne said that he wanted to 'do Poussin over again from Nature' and 'to make of Impressionism something permanent, like the Art of the Museums', he was creating what have become Art-historical clichés; but clichés though they be, the student who cannot form a view of what Cézanne was driving at does not understand very much about painting.

This is why these first chapters will be concerned with that which goes to make up a painting—design, drawing, colour, tone and mass. All these things are part of the mechanism which makes a picture function. But before their purpose becomes plain the elemental starting point of any painting must be defined and discussed. What starts a painting? It does not do for an artist to be too abstract and philosophical about the answer. Matisse in his later years recorded an interview in which he answered questions about the development of his painting as one of the central figures of modern art and was asked what problems were then engaging him. What was he painting now? 'Apples and fruit' answered Matisse. He was lightly insisting on the point that the beginning of a painting is not talent, inspiration, stylistic assurance or aesthetic theory, but quite simply the subject-matter.

Subject-matter is not merely the excuse for a painting; it is the reason for it. It is the fact which every painter has to face at the moment he faces his blank canvas—certainly if he is a figurative painter. He cannot wait for an abstract subject to emerge out of the marks he begins to make as some non-figurative painters do.

It is because I believe that some students treat the subjects of their paintings too lightly, as a mere peg on which to hang some preconceived ideas, that I intend to consider 'subject-matter' as the first element, the prime mover of the artist and his technical problems.

Richard Turner

I Subject-matter

Subject-matter is not the settled thing it once was. Until the Renaissance, almost until the High Renaissance, the subject-matter of all European painting was religious, one might say specifically Biblical. Something of the pagan Hellenistic style was carried into the painting of Byzantine Christianity, but its urbane secular subject-matter was stifled by the disapproval and prohibition of the Church. The Bible (mostly the New Testament) and the lives of the saints, was subject-matter that society insisted be treated with reverence, and the allusions to every-day life that Byzantine and medieval painters sometimes made were slipped in as asides or footnotes to a sacred theme. We can find in some of the Ravenna mosaics exquisitely observed details of animals, urns, draperies and furnishings, but they are subservient to themes of Christ as the Good Shepherd, and to processions of saints. Even the great mosaic of the Empress Theodora and her Suite in San Vitale, one of the grand secular exceptions to the sacred theme, presents the central character as a personage both revering and revered, a figure of saintly status. Christian art never approached the doctrinal rigour of Islam; representation of human and living forms was not forbidden, but art which drew attention to the profane pleasures that might be gained from looking at things was discouraged. Spiritual benefit was the purpose of art; Sir Kenneth Clark has called this attitude the triumph of symbol over sensation. The monastic spirit saw the portrayal of natural delights as subversive, for it held the delights themselves to be dangerous to the soul.

This profound difference of attitude to the subject from our own is of more than historic or academic interest. It happens that the forms and colours of Byzantine and medieval art have a particular charm and excitement for us; they echo that rediscovery of simplicity and elemental statement which characterises a good deal of modern art. Those aspects of the past which seem to provide justifications of our own activities are always attractive to us; Giotto is more spoken of than Raphael, and Uccello rather than Perugino seems to go well with the Van Gogh or Picasso prints on the wall.

This may easily lead a student to suppose that in some way he shares the Byzantine or medieval attitude towards the things he is painting. But, unless he is a dedicated Expressionist, his subject-matter will be of 'profane' and aesthetic, rather than of spiritual significance. Van Gogh had a rare spiritual obsession which gave validity to his ikon-like portraits; but for most painters the dramatised medieval presentation of the single saint-figure in all his symbolic force leads inevitably to the theatrical, and worse, to the sentimental. It is a sentimentality which can be carried over to still-life and landscape. Nothing is more peculiar to its period than is feeling for the subject.

The condition which absolved the painter of Christianity from hunting for his own subject died hard in European Art. The Renaissance added classical mythology to the canon, and it was in this that the painter began to escape from the hieratic demands of dogma and to exercise choice. But he remained bound in other ways. Man as an expression of God became Man as Nobility; indeed the painter often found himself occupied with glorifying the status of particular noblemen or city-states. Even the great church decorations of such Renaissance masters as Tintoretto and Veronese are in effect Venice Triumphant instead of God Triumphant—they are still expressing an ideal, even if it is no longer sacred but secular in feeling.

Among the footnotes of medieval art which did not fully emerge as a subject in its own right until the seventeenth century was that of landscape. The early illuminators might make landscape the setting of their devotional themes, but it took the form of the paradisal garden, the fertile enclosed place in the Biblical wilderness.

Even after the classical Gods and Goddesses of the Renaissance were allowed to recede into the middle distance of Rubens, Claude and Poussin, the landscape remains an idealised classical conception. Velasquez it is true painted (probably on the spot) some small 'plein-air' works which we would call objective, but he seems to have strayed no further than the garden architecture of the Villa Medici.

Many painters, most notably Rembrandt, filled notebooks with objective drawings of landscapes and all manner of observed incidents; but this material remained largely unacceptable as subjects for painting. This is not to say that subject-matter did not enlarge itself throughout the Renaissance and the seventeenth century in other ways than the motifs of antiquity. Scenes of low life became popular in various times and places; but the ostlers of Caravaggio, the beggars and cooking pots of his Tenebrose followers (even of Velasquez himself) retained an air of posed theatricality which was not overcome in the taverns of Jan Steen. Except perhaps in the work of Breughel, it is difficult to find a beggar or a roustabout who is not a little acting the part. It is only in the greatest portraiture, in Memlinc, Holbein, Velasquez and Rembrandt, that we feel ourselves to be in the presence of reality as we understand it.

Perhaps the lesson to be learnt from the sometimes extravagant nature of Renaissance and seventeenth-century subject-matter is that these paintings 'work' because the artists were painting subjects they believed in. I do not mean that Giorgione or Poussin believed literally in classical myth, but they believed in its importance and value. Classical Ideal was not yet mere Antique Fancy. There is a lesson in discovering, too, that it did not always happen this way; while Poussin was expressing a real feeling for Europe's debt to Greece and Rome, the court painters of France—especially a little later under Louis XIV—were turning these themes into bombastic status symbols for the French monarchy; it is impossible to believe that such artists can have had much conviction in the acres of tired, rhetorical canvas which they managed to cover. (Today such courts as survive do not embellish themselves with art, and government pomp lacks the style which even second-rate artists once helped to give it; perhaps an equivalent of official artistic rhetoric finds its modern outlet in the world of advertising.)

Except towards its very close the eighteenth century did not open a new world of subject-matter for the artist. But it did begin to lose conviction in the old subject-matter. It is the first age in which painters really begin to look back upon the 'Old Masters', not only as examples to themselves, but as better than themselves. Even before the death of Watteau (who was perhaps the last expression of the old self-confidence), painting was beginning to alter its Ideal. By the time of Fragonard and Reynolds we may feel that it has in some sense become the purpose of a picture to look like a good picture. It is in subject-matter, as in style, the Age of the Picturesque; and its ingredients lay ready to hand in the work of the earlier Baroque masters. With all its elegance, charm and accomplishment, there is something repressive about eighteenth-century painting. Perhaps it is because painters looked so little further at the world than their predecessors, but were on the whole content merely to affirm what art

19

should look like. The ideal landscape becomes the picturesque landscape to a degree that made possible the success of such landscape gardeners as Capability Brown, who turned whole stretches of land into pictorial parks, complete with ruins. It is a century which produced so many fine painters, and so few (among them Chardin, Canaletto, Hogarth and sometimes Reynolds) who rose above their times. I can think of few eighteenth-century painters who remained wholly within them, and yet created something truly original; chief among these was Gainsborough.

Of course to all such generalisations one can find a legion of exceptions—it is one of the amusements of browsing through the history books of Art—but the student will learn more about the development of visual freedom by looking at the rules which governed the less-than-great painters.

Goya, in breaking from the picturesque and daring to put to canvas and etching plate the real state of affairs, strides from the *ancien régime* to the spirit of republicanism (though he might be surprised to discover himself made a hero of political emancipation). But the nineteenth century took a long time to accord the painter the freedom of subject which Goya heralded. The Age of Reason may have perfected the picturesque, but it was the first half-century of the Industrial Revolution which took it over and made it into bad art.

The blame for the success of decadent and flashy Salon painting which reached its nadir by the end of the nineteenth century is habitually laid on the emergence of the new *bourgeoisie* of industry, rich and numerous beyond the dreams of the genre-painters of Holland, unformed in taste and avid to acquire the hall-marks of gentility; but it cannot be said that cultivated gentility acquitted itself any better.

However, we need not dwell too long on this facet of art. Historically, the significance of the artistic condition in Europe reached by the 1830s is that the best painters were gradually losing their position as the most successful painters. Of course to this there are again exceptions; Ingres, Delacroix and Turner were among those worldly enough to succeed without unduly compromising their art. Yet a comparison of the early with the late work of Landseer shows what might have happened and what in fact did happen to so many talented artists.

Increasingly, the flow of emancipated ideas in art found expression in painters who worked in obscurity or under official disapproval. They were painters for whom public taste no longer provided a professional outlet, men with a few discriminating patrons who allowed them to work as they pleased. It is one of the sad paradoxes that the many painters who revolutionised both subject-matter and our whole view of nature during the nineteenth century were able to do so only because nobody cared. The public reacted to the extent that it fostered sentimentally the new idea of the artist as Bohemian, the rough-clothed dissenter, the smocked, tam-o'-shantered figure of the music halls. But it continued to buy the pictures of Landseer and Meissonier. Constable, who died before the full impact of the new decadence, was among the few who had some public success with his remarkable freshness of vision.

It is our good luck that by 1860 such painters as Corot, Daubigny, Rousseau and Courbet had for long been giving their talents to new truths about nature, because there was nothing (except scorn) to stop them. Their role as 'Independents'—the sort of painter one did not approve of—was even grudgingly accepted by Society. This fortunately gave their work the notoriety, if not fame, to bring it to the attention of students; the young Impressionists were indebted to the example of the Realists.

It was the bold originality of this new generation of painters which finally exploded the old picturesque. As soon as Monet, Sisley and Renoir discovered that beauty could be found by looking at things in terms of the atmospheric space that enclosed them, the ready-made picture scene became irrelevant. Subject-matter no longer had to be about the romantic, the sad, the noble or important; and the shepherd caught in the spotlight in the middle distance could be replaced by the iron railway bridges and suburban boating parties of their own experience. Artists had painted women dressed and undressed for centuries; Degas painted them undressing.

The Impressionists did not only break the bounds of acceptable themes for painters; they made new discoveries and rediscovered the past in ways which I shall talk of later. But, because of them, the artist (and student) is limited only in what he wants to paint by the *passé* look of over-worked subjects. This is not much to quarrel about: the Cubist guitar has had its run for a long time.

The young painter still need not really stray far beyond his neighbourhood. He can paint anything, so long as it is not an unfashionable cliché.

But this freedom is, of course, at once a gift and a problem. The student may wonder if he should draw and paint plaster casts from sections of Michelangelo's *David*; in the old Academies the question would not have arisen—he would have been made to.

It is all very well, however, to say that the student should paint that which interests him; he may not be sure where his limits of interest will lie. What can make a painting? Are there some things that cannot? What subjects will best teach him to discover more about painting and more about subject-matter?

I have no hard and fast answers, but I will put forward some precepts. First, most students are in the quandary of wondering what sort of painter they are— a quandary made the more perplexing by the rapid rise and fall of current stylistic fashions. He must not worry too much about his future image—he can only learn what kind of a painter he will be by painting. He may paint still-life, landscape, the nude, hard-edge abstracts or all of these things, and never paint another after he has ceased to be a student. Never mind, he will only be doing what most fine painters have done before him in this century; these things are part of his experience and will remain hidden elements in his future painting. His important task is to get into the habit of gaining authority over the problems he faces: he will come in time to discover what sort of problems are his (they will not necessarily be the easiest ones), and what sort fail to obsess him—or remain intractable to his talent. 'I have only a little flute, but I try to hit the right note', is often quoted of Corot. But André Lhôte has pointed out that though Corot learnt in time how to paint Corots, he cut his teeth on the disciplines of the Grand Manner.

I do, on the other hand, suggest that the student should paint subjects which help him to learn, and avoid subjects which are works of art already, or whose problems have been so strikingly solved by another artist that mere pastiche will produce a semblance of good painting. Even experienced painters do not always remember that the country parish church, the fine classical façade, no less than the still-life china figurine, are already created works of art; with not too much trouble on the artist's part, they will do some of the job on the canvas which he should be doing himself.

If he can find something new to say about a view of Salisbury Cathedral (Constable did) or the close façade of Rouen Cathedral (Monet did), then certainly he should paint it. Otherwise he may do better to leave them alone, or frankly treat such work as a humble study of what another artist, be he architect or sculptor, has achieved. There is every reason why a young painter should learn from the example of his seniors and his immediate past. But if he looks to another painter for some starting point of method and attitude, he will do well to avoid the other's subjects; this is where the danger of pastiche (the surface aping of style and subject-matter) really lies.

The difficulties of landscape

Many a student makes his earliest serious attempts to paint by tackling landscape. This is a highroad to discouragement. He assumes that landscape is less demanding than other things; in fact realist landscape (as distinct from the symbolised or idealised sorts) is one of the most remotely difficult themes. Landscape requires so many adjustments from the literal facts of nature that it allows alternatives at every stage. In a sense it is not so difficult to draw as the human figure, but no subject makes it so difficult for the artist to stick to the point; let a student try his hand at it, but let it be a testing ground of what he has learnt elsewhere.

I am conscious that such a precept about a universal subject sounds a little tyrannical; I do not want to write anything that would discourage a young painter from doing what he is really excited about. Perhaps I should put it that he should not let himself be discouraged when his results seem at first disappointing.

If landscape poses too many problems, and the ready-made *objet d'art* too few, what should we look for?

Still-life

Still-life is one of the time-honoured, and sometimes time-worn, themes of study. I think it has many advantages. By definition, it stays where you put it, and being an indoor subject it can be seen in a constant light. It can be as simple or as complex as you like. It can be, and usually is, not more than a few feet away; so your powers of binocular vision (stereoscopic vision) are allowed full play. This is most important for it forces you to appreciate that you are dealing with objects in depth. Still-life enables you in an easy and practical way to set yourself isolated and combined problems. It can be made to produce maximum contrasts of shape, texture, colour and tone. *See illustrations 24 and 33.*

The most obvious and useful way to set about this subject, then, would seem to be to arrange material in a pictorial way on a table; this is the traditional way of doing it. It is a perfectly good way, but you must be careful not to over-arrange a still-life. The dangers are these—you may fall into the trap of selecting those objects which you have seen used in famous still-life paintings, and produce a pastiche; you may set up a group which is so nicely and elegantly contrived in placing and colour pattern that it is almost a work of art in its own right. The trouble with such an arrangement is that it can become boring to paint; you may not find much more to say than you have said already in the making of it. But above all the thing to guard against in setting up a still-life is over-refinement. A jug looks very big next to an apple, so you select a smaller one. The spaces between objects seem too uneven—you even them out. Only when you are well embarked on the canvas do you begin to discover that everything is beginning to come out the same shape, the same size, leaving the same gaps. It is not necessary to select things whose juxtaposition is absurd, but they should be strongly contrasted in character, and placed on the table without too much deliberation. Do not then shift things about too much, rather shift yourself (or the table) until an unexpectedly interesting view of the group presents itself. As to background—again do not over-contrive. Still-life often gets posed against a blank wall or a sheet of coloured paper. Such surfaces can be extremely difficult to paint (though this problem must be mastered sooner or later), and it is often better not to construct a box-like space in which your still-life lies imprisoned, but to accept the further side of the room as a natural background. The more you contrive (unless you are a master like Chardin or Cézanne) the more preconceived the activity becomes, and preconception of ideas in painting as in other things means that you are making statements in terms of what you already know. It is not a good way to learn.

There is one common exception to the habit of over-refining arrangements. This is in the matter of colour. It is a temptation to pick out objects which, while they are alike in other ways, are gaily contrasted in colour. Now it is a perfectly good thing to learn contrasts of colour—but not too many. The more that primary and bright secondary tints multiply, the more they tend to cancel each other out. (This is a matter on which I shall enlarge when I come to deal with the attributes and practice of painting in more detail. I must ask the reader to bear with me if I stick to the point of subject-matter for the moment.)

The alternative to arranging a still-life is to find one. I admit that the main difficulty is practical—you cannot expect the remains of breakfast to be left on the table for days. But if you are lucky enough to discover a chance group of objects which is not too vulnerable, or can easily be marked and replaced when you need it, such a group will often provide a freshness and spontaneity of idea which an artificial arrangement cannot by its nature give you. If you do this you must be sure the group you discover is interesting in itself—not because it reminds you of somebody else's painting. You must be sure, too, it is compact enough to be within your limits of vision, and has something about it which is potentially a unity. Nothing is more disappointing than to discover that an apparently appealing subject simply cannot be brought within the limits of the canvas, or that it embraces so many disparate incidents as to be the matter for half a dozen paintings.

You may find that in attempting a still-life of either sort you come upon difficulties which seem insoluble. At this stage it may be profitable to take as a subject a very simplified version of what has been troubling you. Suppose you have been trying to paint a pile of books, an ornately patterned jug and some apples. Try again, but try painting a cardboard box, a cylinder of cartridge paper and some old tennis balls. The underlying simplicities which were hidden under the irregularities, decoration and details of your first subject are likely to become apparent in the more elemental version.

Still-life, if you can make it interesting for yourself, is certainly the simplest field in which to learn, and perhaps the best starting point from which to extend your ideas. The problems of figures, interiors and even landscape are there by implication.

It is, of course, impossible to list all the kinds of subject which can be found. An extension of still-life is the interior; as it is so often the setting for figures and portraits the opposite side of an ordinary room is an excellent matter for study. We have only to look at Van Gogh or Bonnard to see what splendid subject-matter it can be in its own right. If you look forward to the possibility of painting portraits the 'Interior' is an essential study; for it is an old adage that inexperienced painters forget the background of their portraits as they forget the foreground of their landscapes. As with still-life, remember in painting a room what your limits of vision are. As a guide try stretching out your hand at arm's length with the fingers wide apart. The distance from the tip of your thumb to the tip of your little finger will cover about half the width (and height) of your view which you can deal with before getting into difficulties with perspective. This sounds like a piece of somewhat detailed technical advice while I am still talking in general terms, but in fact this question of the limits of vision is basic to the choice of subject-matter. There are good artistic reasons for painting panoramic views if you want to—but remember that special techniques of construction are involved if you start 'taking in' a great deal more than you can see when looking in any one direction. *See illustrations* 10 *and* 13.

The human figure

When you have gained some confidence with static subjects you ought to apply yourself to the figure, whatever you expect to do eventually, for you will find that it makes far more testing demands on you. A man or woman is much more difficult to draw than a flower pot. Considered simply as a form, a human figure (or an animal for that matter) changes with every movement, but does so in a logical way. You may distort or miscalculate the shape of the flower pot without detection, but if you distort an arm or an articulated action you must justify this on artistic grounds, because the literal departure from nature is at once apparent. Then, flower pots have functions but not activities:

a figure does not come to life unless it is doing something. Your figure may be sitting down having his portrait painted, or he may be buying groceries from another figure, and in any situation he will be doing something characteristic of that situation (even if it is only to pose self-consciously while his photograph is being taken). It is hard in the face of this to give any special advice. I would say in the case of a portrait that the essential point to be realised is the sitter's presence. I can best explain what I mean in a negative way. It is natural to wish to make the best of your sitter, and the best of your skill; but if a portrait becomes so flattering, so romanticised and so much a tribute to the painter's virtuosity that the actual mood in the room between sitter and painter evaporates altogether on canvas, then the spectator's belief in the sitter's presence is likely to evaporate too. Practically all the best portraits have been, among their other virtues, records of occasions—occasions when the clients sat for the painters. Other finely painted portraits may fail to convince us that the sitter was ever really there. I do not think that there is any secret road to this, nor has it much to do with style. Perhaps it is mainly a matter of allowing the sitter to establish the character of the painting; paint him as he looks, not as you think he ought to look. It may be partly up to your powers of entertainment to see that he looks at his best—but this is one of the tasks of portrait painting. *See illustrations* 15, 28, 29 *and* 34.

The modern equivalent of the old 'genre' painting poses difficult problems. People in shops, groups of people talking, working, playing, all manner of human relationships are matter for the painter. The practical problem is ever to see them long enough to record the necessary information. The important thing at all events is to catch an authentic moment; a few exact notes are always worth books full of vague sketches. Find if you can events which are frequently repeated by the same people, and notice the characteristic shapes and movements which will also repeat themselves. If you must get a friend or model to pose for further information, do not let the pose become the substitute for the event. Do not rely on photographs or snapshots until you really understand what use to make of them. Degas is supposed to have used photographs for some of his ballet subjects, but if he did, it was not until he had absorbed the whole scene by constant familiarity. Make up your mind whether you are painting primarily the figures, or their setting. One element must play a subordinate role, intimately related to the other. *See illustrations* 10, 23 *and* 25.

The nude

The 'nude' has suffered by being treated as a special subject. As a disciplinary study it has the quality of making the most concentrated technical demands on the painter, and it has long been the basis of art school training. But there was a time in the not too distant past when the nude figure was made so much of a discipline that it became almost impossible to paint. The Impressionists made a point of painting the nude in authentic circumstances—getting dressed, having baths. A nude in a life-room is a profitable subject if it is treated as an event in which the studio plays a part. It is a pity to make a disciplinary parade of 'life-painting'. *See illustrations* 9 *and* 22.

Imaginative painting

Then there is the whole field of what is called 'imaginative' painting (though really all painting should be imaginative.) 'Painting out of your head', to put it inelegantly, is, of course, what most of the Old Masters were engaged in. Today the choice of subjects is personal; and they may be about fictitious events, general ideas, or symbolic moods or beliefs. However, your feelings about the subject should, I think, be clear to yourself, or your painting will be vague in a pictorial sense. You should be able to gather enough information about the shapes and forms you employ to make them seem authentic in terms of the picture, otherwise they will seem improvised and ill managed. Ask yourself if you are painting your subject as well as just illustrating it. If you wonder what the difference is, ask yourself if your painting can convey your meaning without a title. *See illustrations* 7 *and* 18.

Landscape subjects

I have already pointed out that realist landscape is very difficult. But of course it is one of the richest sources of subject-matter, and one of which

28

English painters are particularly fond. It is one of the problems I shall deal with in more detail: but here are a few general thoughts. Of all subjects it is the most vulnerable to picturesque tendencies. Do not search for scenery that looks like a picture. It is in fact a good plan for many painters to find subjects which will be an extension of their other work. It was a saying of the Impressionists that they painted best in the suburbs, and often the best things can be discovered where rural beauty has been tainted with a bit of the everyday world. The landscape painter need not feel he must come to immediate terms with the office block, but he is likely to get more from a huddle of tin sheds than from a thatched cottage. I am not putting forward a 'kitchen-sink' or 'ash-can' attitude, only warning you to avoid the obvious clichés of picturesque landscape. Picturesque views, as well as being clichés, often disappoint in their absence of pictorial quality. Their very obvious beauty and charm makes us forget that we should be looking for something that will go to make a picture within the four sides of the canvas.

When you have found a subject, decide for better or for worse what it is you want to say about it, and stick to this against all temptation. This is of course necessary with any painting, but landscape seems particularly haunted by the ghosts of other painters and will continually offer you a host of alternative possibilities if you give it a chance. These alternatives are not only aesthetic; changes of colour, light, and shadow are constantly throwing out tempting suggestions. *See illustrations* 14, 21, 26 *and* 41.

Whatever your subject may be, and there are endless possibilities, it is worth taking seriously, if it is worth anything. Its nature should set the character of the painting; and, as we shall see, the nature of painting itself is such that you must consider carefully whether or not your chosen subject is truly pictorial. You may well feel that this is an intractable dilemma; I hope that the following pages will help us to escape from it.

II Some attributes of painting

I have named this chapter after a still-life by Chardin called *The Attributes of Painting*. In this he assembled a whole paraphernalia of studio equipment into a monumental group which he organised on the canvas in terms of the classical rules of geometry.

Now not all paintings need to be constructed with the elaborate intellectual logic that Chardin adopted. But in some way or another every painting has to be 'organised'. What does this mean? Let us think in terms of representational painting.

Nature consists of three-dimensional objects in three-dimensional space. A random look at any view of it through a rectangular peephole does not change what can be seen, it merely isolates a part of the view. Framing a bit of nature does not make a picture, which on the contrary is a thing man-made on a two-dimensional surface. Painting is an act of translation from the solid world onto a canvas; this canvas will remain bare until some marks are made on it by human choice. Now it will not do to say that a picture can be an exact imitation of nature in all but depth, which would theoretically involve no organisation.

A camera imitates nature without organisation, but it only imitates a part of nature through such information as light rays are able to record on the film. It is a very small part, far less than painters were recording long before the camera was invented. (Anyone who thinks otherwise is welcome to try painting a portrait from a good colour photograph. He will be surprised at the way in which the information apparently at his disposal evaporates as he begins to work: he will be forced to proceed largely from his knowledge of heads and features.)

The fact is that literal imitation, even of a flat monocular view of nature, is impossible. The painter has only the tonal range that a flat surface can give him (so has a camera). That is to say, that his blackest black is illuminated with the same light as his whitest white; whereas the tonal range of nature can extend from the almost total absence of light of a deep shadow to the full glare of the sun. Even a fraction of nature's tonal range, her mere 'grey day' tone, will almost certainly be more than a painter can match. He must suggest, as it were, a whole tonal keyboard on one octave.

This at once precludes anything more than an imitation of linear accuracy

30

(and on a flat surface even this breaks down after a limited distance from his centre of vision). He must translate, reorganise, select, however closely he wishes to reproduce nature—whether he likes it or not.

But how do you set about translating and organising? How can you reconcile the three dimensions and full tones of nature with the two dimensions and close tones of canvas and paint?

Painting has evolved throughout its history a series of methods for doing this such as line, colour, tone, design, decoration, symbol, and perspective; and by now has accumulated highly sophisticated combinations of such devices. It is because every artist tries to make these combinations according to his own preferences and convictions at the time, choosing his own emphases and omissions, that each artist and each painting is different from the next.

When a painter uses a series of pictorial devices he must try to see them all in relation to each other. I cannot, unfortunately, write about them all at once; but while I discuss some of them in turn, it must be borne in mind that they cannot be treated in isolation during the act of painting.

Design

It might be supposed that I should start discussing drawing as the preliminary to painting, and in a way by writing about design I am doing so. The French word *dessein* and the Italian *disegno* can mean both drawing and design, and indeed French and Italian painters do not separate these conceptions.

'Design' is the way in which subject-matter is ordered within the frame. More specifically it is the method of control which enables the parts of the painting to be seen in terms of the whole. It embraces line, colour, tone, mass, detail—everything in the picture. This is why, for a painter, design must be an integral attribute of drawing. It can also be thought of as a method of decoration.

Another way of putting it would be that design is the means by which the painter arranges what he has to say so that he says it to the best possible effect. The beginner might well think of design as a series of emphatic statements which make him stick to the point.

I cannot lay down hard and fast rules about designing a painting. But I think it usually best to start by looking at your subject and ask yourself what it is 'doing'—even if it is a still-life. If, for instance, a group of objects (or roofs or figures) are sloping towards you—that is diagonally across the canvas—then it may be this diagonal movement which can dominate the design of the painting (see diagrams opposite). Decide where this general direction will cross the canvas. Nearer the top or the bottom? Will the group be entirely inside the picture? Or will it appear from the top left? If you ask how to decide, I can only say you must decide for yourself; you are initiating your picture. A teacher or critic can tell you afterwards, when the painting is finished or well on its way, that your decision was a good one or a weak one. There are methods of adjusting decisions about design, which can relate them exactly to the proportions of the canvas, but these geometrical methods are refinements of ideas, not substitutes for them; they are best left alone by a beginner. *See illustrations* 19 and 30.

Nearly all good designs, I am sure, come out of the subject. This is one of the difficulties of imaginative painting; for it is only too tempting to allow the parts of your picture to arrange themselves simply in terms of a pleasantly balanced design which you have thought of before you have really considered what the picture is about. There is a drawing by a pupil of Rembrandt depicting *The Annunciation*. It is quite a harmonious arrangement, and one would say there is nothing unsatisfactory about it, except that the drawing has been corrected and restated in places by Rembrandt himself. At once, we can see how he has taken the student's composition and shifted the emphasis of placing, so that what was a mere meeting becomes a dramatic confrontation.

In working before nature, you must find the drama in the subject-matter instead of in a literary story. The dramatic in painting is not the same as the theatrical or the sentimental. It is the quality which results when the essential character of the subject-matter has been displayed to its best effect. There is plenty of room for choice in this; where one painter sees drama in colour, others will see it in light and shade, in exactness of shape, or in grand movement.

As time goes on you will naturally find yourself choosing those subjects which spark off the kind of pictorial drama which interests you. But it is not a

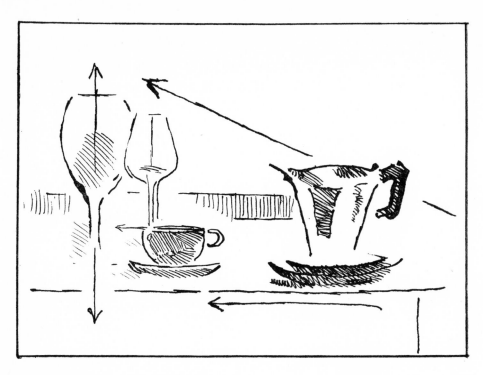

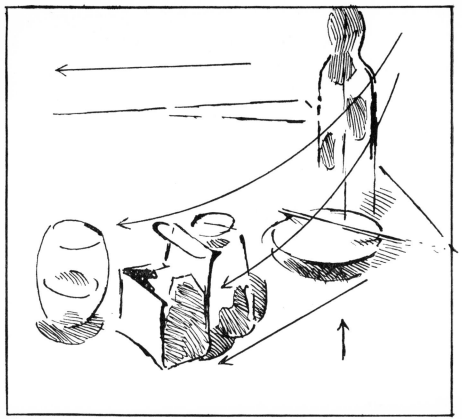

good idea to start hunting too soon to find something in nature which will look like one of your pictures. It is not the way to learn; least of all is it the way to learn about design. (I shall keep reverting to the topic of subject-matter, because this is the point of origin for so much that there is to say about painting.)

Acquire and keep the habit of looking for fresh and unexpected things in order to ask yourself what design is inherent in them, and how they can best be put into order.

I have suggested the instance of finding a diagonal movement across the canvas from some subject which seems to move in this way. The starting point of most pictorial designs consists in discovering a few broad directional movements. Sickert once likened all the possible directions of a line to the moving hand of a clock. A 'movement' can be initially expressed simply by a line drawn at only one such angle; it does not matter whether you think of it as north-east, forty-five degrees east, or half past one. Some lines (even when they do not refer to actual objects) will seem, according to their placing and relationship with other lines, to point to the right rather than to the left, up rather than down (see diagram below). Others will retain their ambiguity. A vertical line raised on

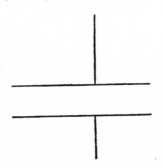 a horizontal will obviously express upwardness and growth, while a vertical dropped from a horizontal will express descent. It is not usually as simple as this; combinations of straight lines in a rectangle will behave in subtle and often unexpected ways. (Our European reading habits lend complexity to composition. We tend to 'read' pictures from left to right just as we read pages. In the Renaissance the theme of processions was popular, and these were usually made to enter the picture from the right, so that the 'reading eye' meets the leading rider and sees the procession pass by, instead of running on ahead.)

But design is concerned with putting facts and intentions in order; while nature may present directions travelling to every part of the compass, we are not likely to get much order on a canvas if we try to reproduce them all. So one of the first tasks of design is to reduce the number of directions which nature suggests. The vertical and the horizontal are the two basic and unequivocal directions which echo the frame, and give a sense of structure to a painting, just as they do to a building. It is less easy to decide about diagonals, but they must not be allowed to multiply too much or the painting will become confused. Cézanne's work shows particularly clearly how diagonals may be reduced to a few sets of directions, all lines within each set being parallel. This practice was common among the Old Masters, but it is not always so easy to detect. A Rubens seems to be all arcs and curving movements, but only because he was adept at covering the traces of his rectilinear structure. One of Cézanne's purposes was to restore such structure to painting, in his own time, by proclaiming it clearly.

As for curving lines—of course they occur in nature all the time and should be allowed to occur in painting. Pictures which consist entirely of straight lines, so that the eye cannot ever 'take a ride', tend to be jerky and brittle. When the eye cannot even move in a curve from point to point along an inferred arc, the effect can be hostile. The Cubists, whose fragmenting and reassembly of forms tended to this effect, would offer the eye relief by introducing some quite clearly recognisable curvilinear symbol.

But curves should not be allowed to travel on for too long. The eye will travel with them so far, and then wander off at a tangent; they provide, as a rule, a weak basis for a composition (see diagram on p. 36). Of course there have been exceptions—such different masters as Tintoretto and Turner based masterpieces on circles and ovals—but paintings which depend on curves for their stability rarely succeed.

I am conscious that I must not use words like 'stability' without trying to define them in some practical way. 'Stability' means to a painting very much what it means to any other structure. A painting cannot literally collapse, explode or skid, like a house, a chemical or a car. But it can seem to the eye to want to do such things. It can be unstable for 'realist' reasons. A man is shown standing in a room perhaps; but the carpet remains a vertical surface—so he has nothing to stand on—and must be either falling or weightless. Or the design may cause instability, so that the eye is carried out of the picture, or can never come to rest within it.

I cannot give any rules for making a picture stable, Geometrical precepts

Diagram after Carpaccio showing surface curves of action. But these are based on an underlying framework of straight lines.

exist, but they can only be applied in terms of the subject. I have already suggested that to fit the subject into geometry is to put the cart before the horse. However, systematic geometry apart, the sense that straight lines govern the main placing of things, though not a rule, is a reliable basis for working. The truest stability will come from your having a central idea about your subject and sticking to it. This is really the essence of design, for your idea provides the material that your design must go to work on. *See illustrations 12 and 17.*

Sticking to the point is not easy, but design is the weapon which helps you to do this. Think in terms of designing your idea from the very start. Let us suppose that you are excited by a landscape in which the foreground pattern leads back across open middle ground to a contrasting pattern of distance. (I am recalling some of Van Gogh's Arles scenes.) Distances are often easier than foregrounds; you may start by placing it somewhere across the middle of the picture, you may only then discover that the essential foreground is out of the bottom of the picture, and that you only get it in by reducing the scale of the distance. We will assume, however, that you have overcome this problem, and have reached a point where you cannot avoid the sky any longer. It may only be as you embark on this part that you begin to realise properly that half your picture is going to be sky—when there was nothing much you wanted to say about it. In short, you will not have designed your idea. If you had thought first, you would have put your horizon somewhere near the top of the picture; however odd a place it may seem for a horizon, it would have been the right place on this particular occasion, and the painting would have been the better for it. Lack of design has in this case led to the painting of two subjects instead of one.

Now a painting cannot be designed simply in terms of line. I have been discussing so far lines which convey the placing and direction of the main parts, not detail. But a picture consists of shapes made of colours and tones (degrees of light and shade). So, as your first idea takes shape, you must wonder how much dark, how much light and middle tone you are going to include. And not only how much, but where. The design or the linear movement, or 'action', of a still-life or a landscape must rapidly transform itself into the design of its forms and colours. The way in which you may set about it is governed by the kind of picture you are painting. 'Action' is common to all painting, but some paintings may have no shadow, others no descriptive colour. I shall be considering the different approaches to representational painting later, and to say too much about their appropriate methods now would be to 'jump the gun'. But my thesis will hold good: that your design must help you to express the main idea you have, whether it be that the reds in a still-life dominate the other colours, or that a sunlit tree stands out against a dark wood. In the one case, the design must allow those objects which give rise to the red their due importance and priority, in the other the tonal point must not be lost by your letting the eye wander from this centre of interest to other tonal contrasts.

There is a point about design I have not yet mentioned only because one cannot say everything at once. And yet it is of first importance, and habitually accorded less importance than almost any other feature of design—not least by beginners. This concerns the proportion of the canvas on which you are going to work. (By 'canvas' I include any surface you are going to work on.) Every subject has its due proportion. It also has its due scale; but if your painting is only half the size you would wish, all is not lost, for most themes can be conveyed on a smaller scale than the ideal (though not always a larger one!). On the other hand if your painting is the wrong shape this can be both frustrating and disastrous.

It is worth taking a lot of trouble to find out just what is the best shape for your idea. We will see what technical trouble is involved later, but first the important thing is to decide what is the best shape. It was again Sickert who pointed out that your idea will extend in shape as far as your interest in it, and that your interest can be trained to fade out, as it were, so as to form the boundaries of a rectangle. It is surprising how well this works in practice. Try making a drawing (without any idea of making it look well) of your 'motif', starting with those central contrasts of objects, colours, masses and actions which gave you the idea. Continue drawing outwards from these until the things you are putting down no longer seem to contribute to the point. You will find that you can draw the lines of a rectangle round, or through, your work with some confidence that it is the right one in the right place. And you may find that you have come to a natural halt because the action of your motif is now related to the corners of the frame. This sort of preliminary reconnaissance prevents you from trudging into the country with a twenty-four by twenty canvas looking for something that will fit on it. If, of course, you have no time to go out and make a drawing, then to come back and prepare the right canvas before going out again—one must say with regret that perhaps you have no time to be a landscape painter.

I am inclined to think that this process of design which discovers its frame by working outwards from the central theme is the most stimulating and least inhibiting for the student.

However, I must say something of the opposite approach, for it must be clear that a great many painters adopt it, and indeed many Old Masters had no alternative but to adopt it. When these masters were given a wall to paint,

38

there was no question of their choosing a proportion; the proportion was waiting for them and they had to work within it. The proportion was an architectural one and the design of the painting executed within it was to some extent understood as an extension of the architecture itself. Now from classical times architectural proportion had conformed to certain ideals, the most famous of which is the Golden Mean. This 'interval' was a basis on which a whole building might be ordered, both as to its overall shape and in its details. It is supposed to have had its origin in the observation of plant and shell growth; the Golden Mean was held to accord with natural or divine law.

A line divided at the point of the Golden Mean is known as the 'Golden Section'. This Section means that a line is cut at such a point that the proportion of the whole line to its larger part is the same as the proportion of this larger

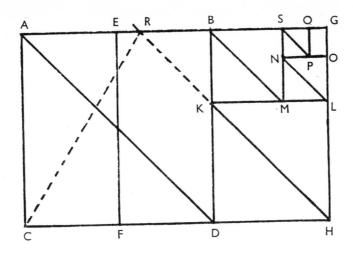

(a) This diagram also shows some additional properties of the Golden Rectangle. A line drawn through HK cuts AG in the Golden Section R. So CRH is a 'Golden Triangle' equal to CBH. It will be seen that AD, RH, BM, NL, SP are all parallel

part to the remaining smaller part. *See* (*a*). To put it simply, a straight line CH is cut at D so that $\frac{CH}{CD}=\frac{CD}{DH}$. This proportion has a useful property. Suppose you extend one side of a square until the extension forms the smaller part of a Golden Section in relation to that side. *See* (*a*). (That is, the side of the square is CD, and the extension DH.) Then extend the square until it forms a rectangle based on the whole line CH. Then you have a 'Golden Rectangle' ACHG, which consists of a square ABDC plus a smaller rectangle which is itself a Golden Rectangle BGHD. You can divide this into a smaller square plus a smaller Golden Rectangle and continue to repeat this process.

The Proportion of the Golden Mean will thus reproduce itself in rectangular form endlessly, either inwards or outwards. Such a ready-made measure or 'modulus' susceptible to all manner of variation, freed the architect from the need to make arbitrary choices about his proportions. His inventions could take place within a logical system of geometry.

The painter, working on a flat surface, found that such geometrical principles of design not only allowed his work to accommodate itself to the architectural surface which he might be embellishing. These principles were, even for 'easel' paintings, a godsend to the artist whose task was to reconstruct biblical and mythological scenes out of his own sense of invention.

So you will find a great deal of Renaissance painting—whether it be by Piero, Raphael or Titian, put into order by a controlling framework of squares, circles, diagonals and Golden Rectangles. Sometimes we may try to read into a painting more geometry than was ever in the artist's conscious mind; but we can see an exponent such as Giovanni Bellini going to extraordinary lengths of ingenuity in order to fit small representational details into a formal framework. This sort of discipline, maintained by Vermeer and Chardin and restored by Seurat, was appropriate to the sort of painter who had the motives and the authority to use it to his own proper ends. But it is a two-edged weapon in the hands of the tyro, and the most probable result of its attempted use will be merely to cramp his enthusiasm. How far in fact is geometry relevant to the painter who works from an observation of nature?

I think he should bear certain things about it in mind. Even though he works

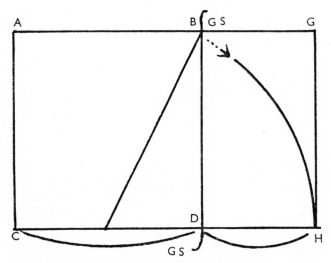

(b) To extend a square to a Golden Rectangle bisect CD. At this bisection strike an arc from B cutting CD produced at H. D is then the Golden Section of CH

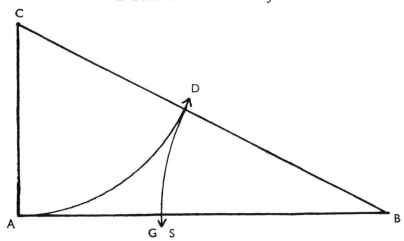

(c) To divide AB in the Golden Section raise vertical AC=½ AB. With centre C, radius AC, cut BC at D. With centre B, radius BD, cut AB at Golden Section

from the centre of his subject 'outwards', so to say, he should remember that the rectangle in which he is working contains in itself some simple geometrical forces. The centre, the bisecting lines, the diagonals—these elements, though not ruled on the canvas, suggest themselves by the presence of the corners. He should remember that a logical proportion of canvas, either geometrical like the Golden Rectangle, or arithmetically simple, such as 'two by three', or 'three by four' is a promising start to a logical design. And certainly he should keep in mind that those subjects in nature which in themselves suggest large geometrical relationships are often the best ones. *See illustrations 7 and 24.*

Drawing

I suggested at the beginning of the last section that drawing (*le dessein*) and design are part and parcel of the same activity. This is true, and yet we tend to think of the word 'drawing' as meaning something else. This is partly because of bad nineteenth-century academic teaching, which pigeon-holed the various attributes of painting in more than name, actually teaching them without reference to each other. But of course 'drawing' has a specific meaning, though probably no two artists would define it in quite the same way.

From one point of view I like to think of drawing as that part of designing an idea which comes to grips with the concrete forms. If 'design' has to do with the placing of a head in a portrait, then 'drawing' is the development and realising of its form. But it is more than that, for the draughtsman takes into account the background to the head, the shoulders and body of the sitter—indeed of the chair he is sitting in; and this all the time he is drawing the head.

So that for the true painter-draughtsman the act of drawing is to move to the particular and concrete from the general and abstract ('design'), but yet in doing so to refer back at every move to the general and abstract from which he started. A tall order!—especially when drawing is more than this for a painter. For ultimately he is not drawing with graphic devices as an end in themselves, like perhaps an engraver or an illustrator: his forms will be resolved in terms of colours. So a drawing is also about where to put his colours, and about the way in which they will explain the forms.

42

Explanation—this is also what drawing is about. Look at any drawing of a figure by Raphael or Rembrandt; it does not merely seem to have imitated a figure, nor does it merely remind you of a figure, it actually explains its shape, so that a solid model (if only a generalised one) could be made from the information contained in that drawing.

I do not say that all good drawing has to be about all these things all the time; it may not be the concern of a drawing to make a full logical explanation where a painter works with entirely flat images. But good drawing contains these attributes where the student does not always suspect it. Copy or trace a figure from a print by Utamaro or Hokusai, whose whole work was geared to the flat pattern-making of the wood block, and you will discover every line of drapery springing from an understanding of the internal form.

Any student of painting who will not be concerned in some way with drawing as an investigation of solid forms is probably storing up trouble for himself—and paradoxically in the field of colour where he thinks himself free. I said at the beginning that we cannot see our subject-matter as the medievals saw theirs: we cannot see colour as they saw it either. They could think of colour on the flat; we can hardly help seeing it in terms of space—the Impressionists put the finishing touches to this. As I write there is a contemporary movement of abstract painters (and it must be agreed a very interesting one) which is struggling with great self-discipline to prevent their colour looking spatial in any traditional way. It is significant that they find this almost insuperably difficult; their colour slips into three dimensions in spite of themselves; the colour of their successes is exciting and novel, but where it is most flat or most ambiguous it is also usually most self-conscious. For us, learning not to read relations of colour as conveying depth is almost as difficult as losing the power to ride a bicycle once you can do it.

The fact is that most painters and students are stuck with a post-Impressionist reading of colour almost as much as they accept perspective to mean depth. Perhaps I exaggerate; you may be able to cast out spatial colour, but if you cannot, you will do well to gain some ability in the kind of drawing which controls spatial colour.

I want now to try and explain progressively some of the devices of drawing

43

which have accumulated from the inventions of the past, and which are now at the disposal of the artist; this preamble is to help you remember that drawing is an integral element in painting.

Symbol

All drawing should have an element of the symbolic. 'Symbol' comes from a Greek word meaning 'token' such as a keepsake or a promissory note. Visually it means a sign by which something is understood. The most primitive form of drawing, both in idea and execution, is symbolic, and consists of a line round a shape. The shape need not necessarily be descriptive in a realistic sense, the line conveys solid representation of nature, although it may well be a shape which recalls an actual object. Conventional signs on maps are examples of symbols. Some such as round dots and circles mean 'towns' of various sorts—if you know the key. Others, such as simplified tree shapes, suggest their own meaning, though each symbol means not one tree, but merely the presence of trees. But a lighthouse symbol, which also suggests visually what it conveys, means one lighthouse.

Now while many symbols in art have abstract shapes whose meaning depends on a code, many more still have been of the sort which suggest their meaning by their shape—the crucifix, Taurus, and the rising sun. Many of these such as the early Christian fish mark, suggest things which are themselves symbols of an idea or a belief. The use of symbols in art has often been extremely complex and esoteric, sometimes sheerly obscurantist, so that when we meet the word 'symbolism' we tend to expect something which is going to be difficult to understand.

And yet a 'symbol' should essentially be the easiest and most instantly recognisable of drawn marks. Symbols may become complex, but they progressively lose their impact as they do so. The simplest and most effective symbol remains simply the line round the shape. This line is the simplest mark of drawing—the first device you acquire. Whether very young children draw symbols, or are trying to imitate, is now a matter of disagreement among the experts; but symbols are what they succeed in making technically.

44

Traditional symbols. (1) is a direct simplification of the actual Cross. (2) is derived from a natural form, but is an arbitrary choice whose meaning becomes recognised by usage. (3) has the same purpose but is abstract. (4) is a simplification of a fish, but its Christian reference is literary and esoteric. A secret sign

The importance of understanding this function of a line is that nearly all good drawings retain something of it. If we wanted to put up a sign meaning 'elephants ahead', Rembrandt's drawing or Bewick's engraving of the animal would each do excellently. Both artists knew that technical skill in drawing forms, textures and details was not quite enough. They must add up to the characteristic shape of the whole. This is why, like the Egyptians, medieval artists showed views of things presenting them at their most clearly recognisable; the side view of a foot and a nose, the front view of an eye, and so on.

Less obvious is the way in which most great painters have done this since, but if you study even such sophisticated painters as Ingres or Renoir you will discover a bias towards this sort of presentation. If you doubt this, compare them with some second-rate nineteenth-century artists, and you will see that this is one of the differences.

Remember that though symbols of the sort which make some outside 'emotive' reference may not appear in your drawings, it is yet worth while asking yourself sometimes whether your drawings could be used as symbols of the objects they describe.

Silhouettes

A line traced round the outside of an object seems to be technically the same sort of line as that round a symbol. Yet it is doing something else. It is actually describing facts about a particular thing. They may be clear facts—the frontal silhouette of a man standing with his arms out is clearly a man—or they may make near nonsense, like an end-on silhouette of the same man lying down.

A line in this sense is really a convenient way of showing how an object

45

may obscure the background. This is what objects do in nature and they can also partly obscure each other. Using lines for silhouettes means studying whereabouts forms will fall within an area, and how they will overlap. Experienced draughtsmen, of course, might begin their drawings with lines which convey both symbol and silhouette.

The important thing about silhouettes is that they are about actual reality; indeed the most familiar kind of silhouette is that perceived as light effect—the man standing in the sunlit doorway makes a silhouette because only his outline can be seen with his cast shadow on the floor.

The making of a silhouette, whether by tracing figures through glass, tracing shadows on walls, using a camera, or just by accurate free copying, is not in itself an artistic act. It is simply the recording of a visual phenomenon. It only becomes art when it is used for artistic purposes, either as symbol or as part of an analysis.

Symbols, then, are kinds of signals which convey meaning because they will be recognised. They are the stuff of which 'conceptual' art is made. Silhouettes are records of particular visual events, and—in the jargon—are essentially 'perceptual'.

Pattern and texture

I mention pattern and texture now, because they seem to be the technical development which follows the simple outline. Many 'primitive' art forms which make no use of modelling or shadow employ the surface marks which appear on varied objects in order to contrast their characters. The pattern of hair, leaves, drapery lines and so on, are used as symbols within symbols to convey the difference between different things and between one part of a thing and another. The 'texture' marks of animals, water, and rocks are similarly used. And, like the symbol, this use of pattern and texture to mean something more than isolated decoration is no preserve of so-called 'primitive' art or hieratic art. It runs through the best work of all periods in varying degree.

At its most elementary it simply decorates and contrasts; it says nothing literally descriptive or anything about solid form. At its most sophisticated, pattern can be used to enhance the rendering of form and to suggest depth. Pattern suggests colour; the kind of colour that simply fills an area with a flat tint.

It is this sort of colour that is appropriate to the kind of drawing I have so far mentioned. Colour, as well as line, can be symbolic; that is to say red can stand for anger, royalty, passion, communism, danger and so on because it has been accepted at various times as a signal for these things. Or, again, the colour red can be used simply to differentiate one area from another yellow or gold area next to it, as in heraldry. 'Gules', heraldic red, is a conventional colour, not an exact tint.

Overlapping and scale

Silhouettes in nature commonly overlap. Overlapping of shapes is not exactly a device of drawing in itself—that is to say it is not a mark, but it is a way of applying marks to suggest depth without the use of light and shade. This kind of three-dimensional inference can be enhanced by contrasts of colour, but will exist when the overlapping shapes are merely outlined. But the rendering of depth in this way depends on the spectator's co-operation.

If you overlap two abstract shapes, you only infer that one is in front of the other; but they may be touching. If on the other hand you overlap familiar representational shapes in a logical way—a seated 'man' silhouette obscuring part of a 'table' silhouette—then the spectator will read into the drawing a sense of depth from his own knowledge of this familiar situation.

It is here that scale comes into play. We know that houses are larger than people. A large 'man' shape overlapping a small 'house' shape therefore means distance from man back to house. Reverse the process, and the man stands behind a doll's house. This depends on a visual acceptance by the spectator of the apparent diminishing scale in nature's distance.

Scale, and sometimes the distortion of scale, is one of the basic items in the modern equipment of representation. (It must be remembered that there are Art Forms in which differences of scale are of purely symbolic significance. In some medieval art for instance a big saint is simply more important than a small saint. There is no spatial comparison.) *See illustration* 35.

47

Sectional lines

The Equator is a sectional line round a globe. Seen edgeways on it is merely a straight line across a circle. Seen from a polar point of view it becomes the outline of the sphere. (Though purists will point out you can never quite see the Equator itself from this point of view.) Neither of these aspects suggests solidity. But seen obliquely the Equator suggests that the circle may be a sphere. It is in this way that an edge or a band (the top of a sock, or a wrist-strap) can be used to suggest the shape of the form on which it lies.

Again, it is a device, which can be used without recourse to light and shade.

You will find sections used to imply solidity in many periods and schools, whose art is otherwise severely formalised. In the Renaissance and afterwards sectional lines became with some artists a conventional way of explaining solidity, and were drawn round the form of nudes in close parallels, where clearly there could be no actual marks of this sort on the figure. Used in this way sectional lines easily become a debased and lazy form of drawing.

Contours and edges

We have seen that an outline can mean a symbol, or a silhouette. It can represent simply an edge between two colours.

But the more that a draughtsman tries to describe his forms in the solid, the more he comes to see that an outline is no longer just a flat silhouette.

He is following an edge which in nature consists of a number of different facets. To begin with, if he is drawing something as simple as the oblique view of a box, he realises that the edges are (in nature) all advancing and retreating in depth. If he is drawing a complex thing like a figure, he discovers that its edge consists of a large number of surface forms overlapping each other, sometimes in very subtle ways. An outline in fact no longer means a sharp edge, but marks the moment when a form (it may be a very rounded form) turns out of view. If he follows one of these edges logically, his line will enter inside the silhouette of the figure, and another edge will appear from behind it. Try pointing across the room with your outstretched hand. In the foreshortened view of this hand

John Hooper

you will easily see the outer edge of your fingers appearing from behind the edge of your knuckle, which in turn disappears behind the back of your hand; this in *its* turn is overlapped by the wrist.

When outlines are made to overlap in this way, responding in greater or lesser degree to the actual relative positions of solid forms in space, they become *Contours*. This is often confused with another meaning of the word used by map-makers: a contour on a map is a line seen from directly above, traced around a constant height—they are therefore what a draughtsman would call sectional lines, each line being drawn through points equidistant from the eye.

The important point about a contour line in the drawing sense (as distinct from the map sense) is that it always disappears behind something else—it can never come back on itself to form a self-contained shape.

The more that a drawing is about reality—about actual solid forms seen in spatial relation to each other—the more outlines must be seen and drawn as contours.

Students' life drawings are frequently seen in which the rendering of the solid form is finished off with a good hard wiry line all round the outside. 'Finished off' in more senses than one, for the continuous outline destroys the sense of the original. The assertive flatness of the silhouette outline destroys the intention of the rest of the drawing.

Modelling: light and shade

The more we draw in terms of the actual forms we see (that is, the more realist we become) the more it becomes obvious that we would not see them at all if it were not for the light on them.

Drawings which are 'conceptual' and formalised, such as those in medieval illuminations, need not concern themselves with this. But a drawing which is highly realist in shapes and outlines—which looks in fact as though it were drawn from a particular model—will almost certainly look incomplete and disagreeable if it conveys no indication of the existence of light on the form. 'Good drawings generate light', said Matisse. The use of shadow on objects

49

in order to explain their forms in terms of light and shade is of the same order as drawing with contours. That is to say, it belongs to the world of realism, and indeed the two devices are used together.

If you examine the drawings of great masters you will see that the shadow (or 'shading') in them is clearly not a mere imitation of surface light and shade effects. The marks which mean 'shadow' are introduced in order to enhance the explanation of the forms. You will usually find that the shadows are emphasised, or at least drawn in most particular detail, where the forms turn from one plane to another; they start, that is, from somewhere inside the form and approach the outline. They are not seen from the outline (or contour) inwards. It does not matter too much what sort of mark goes down to suggest shadow: it is very important that they should be in the right place, and should be selective. The fact that two-thirds of a torso is in light and one-third in shadow is a big fact. The little shadows that are caused *within* the light part by minor bumps and depressions are small facts. Some of them will be structurally important and cannot be left out, but they must not be emphasised so much as to destroy the lightness of the light side. This should never be forgotten; forms can be 'modelled' all over to such an extent that they become in effect bas-reliefs, not explanations of solid shapes. Modelling is the notation of where the form turns away from the source of light. If this modelling of a head does not convey light, the result may be a map of the marks on the face rather than a drawing of the form.

A secondary kind of shadow is the 'cast' shadow. One object interrupts the light which would otherwise reach another form, and casts part of its own distorted shape on that form. These cast shadows are useful where forms join each other—arms to bodies and so on—and where large forms need relating. The total shape of a figure and a chair will cast its combined shadow on a wall and floor, and this fact can be used. But they can be the most destructive of all drawing and painting devices when badly used. A cast shadow is not in itself anything; it is simply an absence of light. This is where the camera inexorably fails; it cannot distinguish between the reasons for shadow. As soon as you make a cast shadow more important than the things that are causing it you are really behaving like a camera; and this is one of the reasons why works done in disguise from photographs, even with all the ingenuities of modern filtering and developing to help, invariably betray themselves.

Reflected lights. These are an additional effect of nature, which can enhance the form of a drawing; most draughtsmen respond to them and indicate their existence. But, like cast shadows, they can be dangerous if made too much of; shadows should not be so filled with reflected light that they cease to be shadow.

(1) *Silhouette of a dog, traced from a Carpaccio painting.* (2) *The main contour lines of the same painting. The overlapping fur lines of the back suggest sections round the form.* (3) *A sketch of the main light and shade masses of the same painting*

The word 'shading' is a good word spoilt. It has come to imply special techniques for putting in shadow, with a pencil or some other tool. Leonardo's parallel silver-point lines, for instance, have a great appeal which students have often tried to imitate. But there is no point in imitating other people's 'hand-writing', for this is what such marks are; a painter should always remember that what matters is the quality of drawing in his painting. Drawings deliberately made to look well are usually tedious. So do not waste time trying to make shading that 'looks good'; you may actually succeed, and this will only mean that your drawing becomes a lazy substitute for looking.

In its fullest sense, the study of form in light cannot terminate at the edge of an object or figure. The more reality the object is given the more it needs to be shown as existing in a real world. An apple in a child's alphabet can be a symbol on a piece of white paper, but a real study of an apple demands something about the plate or the table, for real apples do not float in space. So it is with figures, furniture and everything.

It follows that you should look at the tones, lights and shadows of nature round the things you are drawing. Sometimes you will see the shadow on one thing disappear into an equal shadow on a surface behind it. Note this by letting the shadow of your drawing 'travel through' from one form to the next, because this is a necessary factor in tonal painting.

'Local Colour'—the tint of individual objects—can be stated in a drawing, but it is best made much of in drawings which have least to do with shadow. That is, a figure in full light can be shown easily to have black hair, but seen against the light, the same figure is in silhouetted shadow, and it is very difficult to make dark tones mean both shadow and local colour in one drawing. So, let your drawing 'prefer' one sense or the other.

If you are interested in flat areas of local colours, stick to views of your subjects which display the least possible shadow and you will then avoid this quandary. If, on the other hand, you want to explore the dramatic contrasts of light and shade—'chiaroscuro'—then you must only hint at the local colours of things, because these colours are modified as they cut across the tonal 'masses' of the drawing.

As an example of the first sort of drawing, look at the best Japanese Ukiyo-ye masters such as Harunobu, Utamaro and Hokusai. These artists, who drew for the wood block, managed to convey a marvellous sense of form and movement without any reference to shadow at all. There is sometimes a sort of tonality in the flat colours, but the solidity is arrived at entirely with contour, pattern, and subtle hints of scale. These are used in a way which combines observation with formality; the objects never become so literal that the eye demands any shadow. With their rigorously limited means, these artists produced drawings as inventive technically as any that have been made. When in the mid-nineteenth century photography reached Japan, and artists tried to compete by introducing shadows into their prints, the whole tradition collapsed.

Look at drawings and prints by Rembrandt and Goya to see the opposite technical approach; you will see that local colour would be an intrusion, almost an impossibility in these works. They clearly lead to a sort of painting in which colour has to take account of the illumination of forms. *See illustrations 37, 38, 39, 40 and 41.*

Colour

As a poet uses words, a composer notes, so a painter uses colour—it is his language.

This was always clear to the apprentice of the Old Master; grinding the Master's colour was probably one of his first jobs. It is clear to most modern students, who are encouraged to approach their training as painters or designers through colour experiments. But a long period of academic training in art schools ended, not so long ago, during which a student might be expected to spend two or more years drawing before ever being allowed to hold a brush. Their drawing, which became often highly skilled, also became an end in itself; such students might well approach colour with inhibition.

Colour is not in fact an unwelcome intrusion on drawing, it is the very material with which the artist draws and designs.

I have already said that colour can be used symbolically to represent ideas. But this is not the way in which the realist painter usually sees colour in the first place.

We might start by thinking of colour as we see it in nature. In nature grass is green, tomatoes red, lemons yellow. When we come to different human races we refer to them less accurately and more conventionally as white, black, yellow. If we have to describe more precisely in one word the colour of a 'white' face, we probably say 'pink'. All these are the 'local' colours of the objects. They are the colours we know them to retain in their make-up at night or in a dark room. When materials are dyed they receive a local colour. But we do not always see them like this. It is our common experience that green grass—the same sort of green grass—looks quite different as it recedes into the distance. In the far distance it will be blue or grey. This is because successively thicker veils of atmosphere interpose filters which cut out the yellow element of green.

But look at a lemon on a white plate. It is yellow. Think about painting it in a realist way, and this no longer seems quite true. We do not cease to believe that it is yellow all over, but we *see* that the highlight from the window is not yellow, but *almost* white with perhaps a touch of violet. The shadow is not yellow but very dark—until a reflection from the plate lightens this with a cold grey. Even the light part is not the same yellow everywhere, but varies from rich to pale.

All these are illuminated colour, colour modified by light falling on a solid form which catches it at different angles, and reflects according to its textures. In some places the form does not catch the main source of light at all, and is illuminated by other objects. Texture modifies colour optically; surfaces which are rough continue to catch the light as they turn into shadow far longer than smooth surfaces. As a rounded surface passes from light to shadow it becomes greyer and colder, becoming warmer again as it enters the dark shadow. This phenomenon may be modified by the circumstances of lighting—by cold reflected lights, by brightly coloured surrounding objects illuminating the half-tones. But it is *not* modified in principal by the local colour of the object itself.

So now we have two sorts of colour, local colour and illuminated colour. To these we must add another: induced colour.

Induced colour is the element of change which appears in one tint because of its proximity to another. The three primary colours, yellow, red, and blue, are the most stable and resistant to induced colour. The secondary (or binary) colours—green, orange, violet, are pretty stable but can be modified slightly by a primary. When we come to colours which are duller and more broken admixtures, right down to grey, we find that they can be progressively altered in appearance by brighter colours placed round them, or next to them.

Now this is a phenomenon always understood and exploited in an empirical way by painters. The science of the subject began to be investigated systematically in the late seventeenth century, but it was the theories of Goethe and Chevreul which drew the notice of painters.

54

Chevreul was a scientist who was concerned with improved colour in the Gobelins tapestry factory in the first half of the nineteenth century, and as a result of his researches he produced a book on colour which commanded much attention from the Impressionists. Chevreul's principles have been refined and to some extent replaced by modern research; and he himself did not properly understand their application to painting. But he did propound a 'law' which holds good in practice—that of Simultaneous Contrasts. This sounds alarming, but can in fact easily be verified with a few bits of coloured paper.

He knew that sunlight can be divided into the spectrum—its component parts. The dominance of the primary colours in the spectrum can be placed in a circle like a sliced cake. Presented in this way, the yellow segment would occupy very roughly one-fifth of the circle, the red one-fifth, and the blue the remaining three-fifths. Any diameter line will then touch the perimeter not only at opposite points but at opposite colours. That is to say a line drawn from the very middle of blue (pure blue) will hit the other side at the reddish end of yellow, i.e. orange. So pure yellow has as its opposite violet blue, pure red is opposed to greenish-blue. These opposite colours are called complementary colours.

Now Chevreul said that any colour bright enough to have a distinctive hue will throw an apparent film of *its own* complementary onto a more neutral colour. Of course a large amount of a very bright primary colour will have the maximum of influence on a smaller internal bit of a very neutral colour.

Try cutting 'windows' in pieces of red, yellow and blue paper or card and then place all these on one large piece of grey paper. In the red card the window will appear greenish, in the yellow it will be rather violet, and in the blue a warmish orange. The differences are, of course, an illusion in the sense that the local colour of the single piece of grey paper will not have changed; but the apparent shifts of colour can be astonishingly distinct. The principle holds good in more subtle ways. A dominant warm green (i.e. yellowish) will make a subsidiary cool green (i.e. bluish) even more cool by imposing a note of violet. Chevreul tabulated pages of combinations of this sort: but it is best to conduct your own experiments—you will soon find that you can predict the sorts of change that will take place.

All this is only in itself a natural phenomenon; it is not art. But it is important, because if the painter cannot command his colours, these optical changes will occur in his painting when he does not want them to. For colours are not necessarily enhanced by contrasts: a 'tint' which seems 'clean' in its place on the canvas can become inexplicably 'dirty' as the work progresses without its having been touched. The explanation is that it has had, as it were, a film of colour placed over it by another colour. A cool green with a film of blue violet may look purer, but if it gets a film of orange it may 'lose its life'. It does not do to get 'theory bound' about colour; all these principles will not create a good picture for you. But some knowledge of how colours behave does help a great deal in putting them to your own purposes, in both a positive and negative way.

These rules can be the subject of tricks. We have all seen paintings, or posters, or material, in which two brilliant complementaries are exactly matched in strength—usually in stripes. Since neither can impose its will on the other, the result is an unstable, dancing dazzle which can be an assault on the eyesight.

Tone

Each colour possesses not only a true (blue, yellow, brown) but a tonal value. This is its degree of lightness or darkness from black to white. When we talk of a 'colour value' we mean this combined quality of a colour.

We have seen that tone in nature has a great range from light to dark, compared to which the whitest canvas to the blackest paint is contained in a small range. One of the problems a painter must face is that of regrouping the multiple values of nature not only in their lines but in their tones so that he can deal with them. He must arrange them in sets so that a number of middle tones in nature have to join one family on the canvas.

Like everything else in painting, colour values and their manipulation can only be controlled by practice. This is why I want to describe some of the various approaches to colour when I discuss the more practical problems of painting. I will only add now that any student who wishes to acquire a full sense of colour had best learn to use it in a formal way, that is to describe, with values, the shape of things in space. Colours which are a mere decorative addition to a basically monochromatic idea can be very pretty, but they always have the disadvantage of looking a little arbitrary, of making people feel that some other colours might have done equally well. As Cézanne said, 'When colour is at its richest, form is at its most complete'. As an attitude it is a good point of departure. *See illustrations 11 and 16.*

Perspective

Perspective systems are the various ways in which we project what we see onto a flat surface. The common form used by the representational painter is Central Perspective, and a section describing its simple principles (from which the rest can be worked out) is given on pages 112 and 113. I also discuss some of the general problems involved in dealing with perspective.

Emphasis

I include this as an attribute of painting. I might have called it 'choice', 'decision' or 'selection'. It is that element in a painting which shows that the artist has chosen between one possibility and another. It shows that he has asked himself the following sort of questions, and found answers. What exactly is the most important thing in my painting? Which are the dominating planes—the flat-on surfaces or the receding surfaces? Which colour do I emphasise as the most important? How much of the painting must be light, how much half-tone, how much dark?

If you start thinking about all the questions you *could* ask yourself, you will see that they provide a very good reason for keeping your ideas simple! Do not take on themes so complicated that questions like this cannot be answered. It almost certainly means that you are trying to paint two or three pictures at once.

Painting consists of making decisions and emphasising them in due order. To weigh every consideration is what makes painting difficult—but it is much better to make even wrong decisions than no decisions at all.

III Approaches to the technique of painting

I have tried to provide the reader with advice on two kinds of equipment—a material equipment of paints and brushes and a theoretical equipment for forming pictorial ideas.

Now I want to discuss their practical application by describing some ways in which we might actually set about a subject.

(a) 'Tonal' still-life

Let us set up a simple still-life indoors. It should be lit from *one* source (i.e. it should not be receiving illumination from opposite windows), and you should place yourself so that you are looking rather more on to the light side than the shadow side of the still-life. Not more than one very bright colour should be introduced—it might come from green apples, oranges, lemons, tomatoes, or anything you like—but stick to one such source of colour. The other things should be more reserved: stone jars, cardboard boxes, bare wooden table tops —any simple assortment of objects and surfaces which make a muted contrast of warm and cool tints. You might introduce *one* other brighter colour which may contrast with, but not compete with, your main colour accent.

If you are going to approach the colour of this subject in a tonal way, this means that you must look at the light and shade falling on the whole subject in order to see what sort of a pattern it makes. You must study the way in which the light makes some surfaces warm, others cool. You must notice how far this contradicts the local colour of the objects. You must also, of course, consider the linear placing of the still-life—what shape of canvas do you need for the design?

All this suggests that it might be well to look before you leap. I am an advocate of the preparatory drawing, because I think it does not inhibit painting, but rather releases it. So before you think about a canvas, make a number of drawings of your subject to the same scale. I like to do these on very thin paper, even tracing paper, so that one can be laid on another. Let one drawing discover a broad vigorous rhythm of main directions, another the masses of light and shade, a third a careful rendering of silhouettes and details. It should be possible to trace from these a 'master drawing' which will provide the framework for your design, and which will tell you what proportion to work on.

Now you can start to assemble your materials. Let us assume that you have stretched a white primed canvas—if it is not the right proportion you can mask off a strip of one side with some neutral coloured paper. Put your canvas at eye level on your easel, tipped forward a little so that it does not shine, but in the full light of the window. We said earlier that light falling almost edgeways on to a surface produces a 'cool' or grey effect: this is equally true of your canvas. Do not give your painting an artificial unity by painting in a cool half-light; it will disappoint when you move it. Whether you are sitting or standing, I recommend placing your palette on a table of appropriate height in front of you; this keeps you from painting with your nose against the canvas, and leaves you free to mix your paints properly. You will initially need:

> *Flake white or zinc white*. Titanium is a very good white but so powerful a 'cover' that a little of it tends to flood other colours with its own whiteness. Introduce it gradually to your palette.
>
> *Yellow ochre*—an opaque colour.
>
> *Light red*—an opaque colour.
>
> *Ivory black*—a semi-transparent colour.
>
> *Raw umber*—a semi-transparent colour.

This is an austere but traditional palette with which to start a tonal painting. It is simple; it gives you a range from light to dark and from hot to cold and the primaries are suggested without being asserted. The pigments mix readily together.

> A selection of long round hogs—say sizes 2, 4, 6, 8, two or three of each. One sable of medium size. (This can be mislaid without disadvantage at this stage!)
>
> A palette knife. This should be used, as it is named, on the palette, *not* on the painting.
>
> Genuine turpentine (NOT *turps substitute*). Pour out what you need in a dipper

or a tin. Keep the cap on the bottle to prevent the turpentine becoming sticky. Do not use old air-exposed turpentine or add fresh turpentine to yesterday's treacly remains. Keep if you can a stock of clean empty tins from the larder—to use and throw away.

A supply of rag. A humble but essential item of equipment. Without it you cannot keep your palette clean.

Monochromatic tone

If you are about to attack the subject from a 'chiaroscuro' or light and shade point of view, there are some obvious disadvantages in starting on a white canvas. You are right at one end of the tonal scale, and almost any mark you put down will look initially very dark. The tonal painters before the Impressionists in fact started on a toned canvas. But the canvas should always be basically white, otherwise it will darken the paint on top. So at this stage a very transparent middle tone can be laid on the white ground by rubbing in a thin layer of raw umber and turpentine. Mix these rather dark so that the umber becomes a middle tone of very thin rapidly drying pigment as it is rubbed over the canvas and the surplus picked off by the brush. If the result is too dark and rich, rub the canvas down with some rag.

From your drawing you will now be able to mark on the canvas the principal points and directions of your composition—if the raw umber ground is thin (lean) enough you need not wait for it to dry. The marks can be made also in umber—but not as a series of black lines. Your drawing should be dark enough to show where the paint will go, no more. You are going to use black to mean deep shadow, so do not start by using it to mean something else. Avoid in fact making a series of very assertive linear shapes at this stage which do not represent the areas of tone the picture will finally assume. It will give you a false idea of the design. At this stage, when you have a toned canvas, and enough light marks to give you confidence in the placing and shapes of the motif, you should ideally leave the work until it is surface dry. When you resume, pour out some fresh turpentine and add a little linseed oil. No one can lay down the law about the ideal medium—it is a matter of individual preference—but it is a good principle to start 'lean' (i.e. thin pigment, little oil) and end 'fat'

60

(rich thick pigment, more oil). In the initial stages there will be enough oil in the tube, and depending on the colours you may not need to add oil to your paint at all, but merely to use less turpentine.

The second stage of the painting should lay in broadly the pattern of light and shade in the design. A traditional procedure is to put down a dot of pure white for the lightest thing you can see, and a dot of black for the darkest. This reminds you of your tonal range, though you need not use it all. Now see how much of your subject looks about half-way between light and dark—if necessary trace lightly on your canvas with a thin grey line every part that falls within this category. Mix on your palette with your knife a generous amount of raw umber mixed with just enough white to bring its tonal value up to this 'half-way' point. The white will tend to make this mixture cold and you can put in a little yellow to restore the 'warmth' of the umber. Now rub in this mixture, again very lightly and thinly, across all the 'half-tone' part of the subject. The paint need only be a little less thin and transparent than the original toned ground and unless you made the ground too dark in the first place you will find this half-tone a good deal darker.

All this activity is so far monochromatic; we are simply trying to find the broad tonal pattern of the painting.

Between the value of the half-tone and of the black dot try to establish in a similar way two more successively darker tones. On the 'light' side of the half-tone place two successively lighter tones. If your eye has been taking in the subject broadly enough, you will now find that you have about covered the canvas with the white, the black, and five intermediate tones; the original toned ground will function as one of these values. These tones will not coincide with the objects, but will form shadow areas running across their edges. In other parts the 'tone' will represent the 'local colour' of an object, for this may happen to coincide in tonal value with a shadow area.

The result of all this may look a 'bit of a mess', or at least more like an abstract than a representational painting; but do not worry. You are laying the foundations for simplicity and breadth, and you can at this stage touch in again lightly some of the linear statements about the objects which you originally put in. Some of these will no doubt have been lost in the process of laying in the tones. These outlines can be broad and simple; but, I repeat, *not too black*, or they will look like tone values. Particularly do not draw outlines, sharply, right through shadow areas.

You will now have a monochromatic representation of your subject, with all the different tone values of nature reduced to seven on your canvas. If you find that you have not been firm enough but have allowed all the nuances of nature's light and shade to mislead you into putting down, not seven, but twenty-seven, different values—now, and not later, is the time to act. *Reduce your tones into these simple groups*. I have said seven; ten perhaps, though you may find as few as four sufficient.

A technical digression

I must intrude on this with a boring technical point, for this is the moment at which it must actually be dealt with when you are painting.

First, you must again give your canvas time to dry. Raw umber, if you have been using this as your basic monochrome, dries quickly; so that unless you have put in too much white, or laid the paint on too thickly, your canvas should be ready to work on the following day. If in correcting and re-stating you have used too much paint for this stage, scrape it down with your palette knife. If you are gentle you can take off the surplus pigment without removing your essential underlying statements. Do not rub down with a rag unless you want to remove a passage altogether.

Secondly, proceed at once to scrape down all the surplus on your palette, and rub it clean. Do not try to economise. A clean palette is vital, and while you can keep the 'blobs' of pure paint round the side from day to day, the work-centre *must* be clean. Never be short of a mixing surface.

Thirdly, *wash your brushes*. Rinse them out in your surplus turpentine (which you should then throw away), and wipe off the surplus pigment very gently on a rag. Then wash each brush separately in cold or lukewarm water, with ordinary household soap (NOT a detergent) rubbing the paint out on the palm of your hand. You must get the paint out right up to the metal ferrule, and you can safely splay out the hairs of a hog against your palm in order to do this. The brush is not clean so long as it is colouring the soap lather. Rinse it

62

thoroughly, *shaking* out the water—do not try to squeeze it out. Do not dry brushes in front of a fire.

Finally, wipe your palette knife clean and clean out your turpentine container thoroughly.

I make no apologies for this somewhat governessy advice; these humble activities are part of the actual job of painting a picture. They are not things that can be left till later; indeed a great deal of the trouble that students have with colour and oil paint comes from battling against the hopeless odds of dirty palette and brushes.

Colour values

Assuming that your canvas is now dry, you can now consider the tone values you have put down and begin to wonder what they mean in terms of colour.

So far you have been reducing everything to monochrome. You have not been doing this as a camera would, because you have been grouping tones into sets, and have been making choices about this. Nevertheless, you have used essentially only one of your limited palette of colours, together with a little white.

It is surprising what a long way yellow ochre, light red and ivory black will carry you in the next stage. You will remember that surfaces edgeways on to the light tend to be grey and cold. Look at your subject and you will find that this is so. Half-tones which are caused by a 'turning away' from the light will mostly be cool, even on warm objects. Try turning the face of a red or orange book gradually away from the window and you will see this coolness creep over it.

I suggest now that you take the 'middle value' shapes—those which you first filled in over the drawing—and start to paint in all those passages which seem to you 'cool' because they are deflected from the main light, without being quite in shadow. Take care that these greyish colours you put in are of the same *tone* as your umber underpainting.

You will find that you have begun to 'model' the subject with colour, and that you have been putting the colour 'values' down of a number of surfaces which share something in common—their direction to the light. These values can be placed quite simply and flatly on the canvas with opaque paint, thick enough to cover the underpainting solidly. There is no need to load the canvas with chunks of heavy impasto, nor on the other hand to 'smooth' on to it a sleek layer of graduated shading. Think of pieces of mosaic which have to be slipped into place. Let the texture take care of itself at this stage. Nothing looks worse than meaningless 'brushwork', and you will find that the quality of your paint and of your brush strokes will develop as you gain confidence in your intentions.

You might now strengthen and restate in their warmth (for they are usually warmer than half-tones) the full shadows. You may need to add to your palette a burnt umber or burnt sienna—but do not let the shadows become 'hot'. You will find gaps on the canvas between your half-tones and your deep shadows. These are the intermediate tones and as you study these parts of your subject you will find yourself similarly assessing their values. Colours which seem very puzzling in quality when you try to paint right round a jug or an apple in one go, become much more easily definable when you compare them with similar colours elsewhere.

As you start building up the values on the illuminated side of your subject you will come upon surfaces which have much more 'local colour' value. Do not be afraid to try and state these colours as they are; only be careful not to put down more of this sort of colour than you can actually see. It is surprising how little of an apple is actually just 'green' in the light. Again be careful not to disrupt the simple tone values of the underpainting. You will find that passages which hardly explained themselves in the under-painting, because of common tone running from one object to another are different. Warm and cool colours of exactly the same tone value can be played against each other in your painting as often as you can discover them in nature; paradoxically nothing establishes the effect of depth more firmly in a painting, than this.

On this topic of comparing tones, I give one 'tip'—which by now almost suggests itself. Compare dark tones with other dark tones, light tones with other light tones, in order to establish both their value in nature and their place in your tonal design. If, and it seems apparently easier, you compare a light with a

Peter Millband

dark you are still forced to put down a limited tonal equivalent on canvas. The next time you do this you may choose a different equivalent. The two lights you have put down will be lighter than the dark passage all right, but they may be reversed in relation to each other. Compare them to each other in the first place and you will not fall into this trap.

If, as I suggested, you set up a group which allowed one bright colour to dominate, say a lemon for example, then it is a good plan to put down a firm 'note' about its brightest quality before you start embarking on the lights. This might be a blob of almost pure lemon yellow mixed with a little cadmium. It may look startlingly brilliant against the umbers and cool greys of the darks, but it will give you a colour to work towards, just as the white and black blobs gave you tones to work towards. You will be able to define with confidence the warmth and 'yellowishness' of more muted ochres and browns, because you can see how bright these can be allowed to grow. 'Local colours' must take second place to illuminated colour in tonal painting, but there is always the risk of your stating them so subtly that at a few feet from the canvas they are indistinguishable.

You will discover that you can be very bright about local colour in a tonal painting, as long as you can decide *which* colour to make much of and to stick to it. Difficulties start when you try to render bright oranges, reds, and blues together with a complete range of light and shade. The early 'chiaroscuro' painters did not quite get over these difficulties, and attempts to paint portrait heads in romantic lighting on top of heraldic panoply of uniforms and orders occurred in such very accomplished work as that of Van der Helst, the seventeenth-century Dutch painter. The result was not satisfactory. It was Rembrandt who really discovered, or at least exploited, the principle that light excludes colour. Very bright light actually does cut out most local colour (as you will know if you have looked at a midday landscape in the Tropics), so this is not merely an artistic convention. One is confident that all the colour values in Rembrandt are illuminated; in a Van der Helst half of them are decorative additions.

However, this is something of a theoretical aside, and I am trying to be practical. A few words about the paint surface. We have seen that we start a tonal painting 'lean' and end 'fat'; this should be technically so of any oil painting. It is good physically and makes for permanence, because under-layers of pigment tend to suck the oil out of succeeding layers. If you do not supply this oil with richer top layers, then the effect of 'sinking' takes place—where the colour values become matt and lifeless. And in time, as paint 'saponifies' or tends to transparency, underlying colours will show through upper layers. Above all, of course, a thin top layer is in danger of being cracked by a thick under-layer.

As well as physical, there are good artistic reasons for keeping the *darks* thin and underlying, while the lights are built up on top. Look at your still-life again and you will see that the shadows seem to have absorbed most of the light and colour, while the light parts are reflecting the light and colour back at you. If you put a thin smear or 'rub-in' of transparent black or umber on your canvas so that the lighter ground just shines through, you get something of the optical quality of a shadow—the light goes through the pigment to the ground, and is absorbed by the pigment. Solid paint reflects light straight back to you; this is very well for the light parts of a painting, but clearly bad for the shadow parts. In some Old Masters you will find a subtle game played between transparent black paint, meaning shadow, and opaque black paint, meaning a black coat or dress in the full light.

Sickert, whose various writings are full of 'good tips', once likened a good paint surface to a pack of cards dropped on a table. Drop a number of cards—these are the underpainting. Then drop more on top of them—these are the half-tones; they will partly obscure the underpainting. Another layer—the lights. Yet another—the high-lights and brilliant accents of colours. Each layer partly covers what came before, yet each in places shows through to the ground.

I do not say that all paint surfaces must look like this, but very many painters have conducted themselves through this process. I do not know of a better way in which to learn the 'grammar' of painting.

This process—the light drawing on a transparently toned ground, the monochrome, the laying in of the cool half-tones, the working on either side of these towards lights and shadows—may seem to have the disadvantage that you are always making comparisons of values instead of painting *things*, the objects that interest you. It is true that 'developed', 'well-conducted' painting of this sort does insist that the objects emerge in their identity through the gradual process of painting. You may ask of it—when is it finished? Cannot this process of painting go on until every tiny plane and facet containing its own 'value' has been stated, that is pretty well for ever? In theory, yes. In practice, 'emphasis' takes over, and we bring our concentration more and more to bear on the main theme, until we feel that we have said what we wanted to say, or at least, as much as we can say. A tonal painting is, in a sense, never 'finished', but it will look 'complete' if the painter has done what he set out to do.

I do not want the reader to suppose that I have described a hard and fast method of setting about the painting of light and shade; it is merely a possible one which has many variants, both in order of working and in the colours used. Rubens, whose sketches are perfect demonstrations of the art of developing a painting, started on a transparent grey ground and swept in a golden ochre underpainting. You can usually find the silver grey half-tones on the turn of forms clearly stated, as you can see the progressive thickening of pigment towards the lights. You will no doubt find your own personal variation, and with practice you will perhaps be able to make the monochrome stage more summary; though a tonal painting which is supported on and built up from some degree of reserved underpainting is almost always the richer for it.

It is fashionable now among critics to decry 'tonal painting' as though it were a peculiarly English vice; but in fact you will find that it formed the basic student work of such French modern colourists as Matisse and Bonnard. You will certainly learn how colour 'functions' in a formal way, and I think that an understanding of tonal values is always implicit in the work of great colourists. *See illustrations* 8, 11, 16 *and* 32.

(b) Painting according to Impressionist principles of colour

The Impressionists did not abandon tonal painting but modified it. One thing that worried them was that tonal painting had become a matter so much of designing in terms of light and shade that it was difficult to give the actual shapes of objects their true importance. This was particularly true of landscape; the contrived chiaroscuro of Romantic landscape clearly did not correspond to what happened in nature. The movement of dramatic cloud shadows was not actually held in suspense for the convenience of the artist. They developed a method of using colour which had already been indicated by Constable, Corot and the Barbizon painters. Colour Theories such as Chevreul's led them to see that in sunlight a bright local colour would cast its own complementary onto its own shadow areas. Thus, the duller shadows inside and behind the bright warm green of a tree could be seen as violet grey. The half-tone greens would tend in this direction and thus become cold greens. They elevated this into a principle—disposing of the dark warm shadow convention and substituting the complementary colours.

This allowed them freer rein with the bright and clear tints of landscape— every colour has its shadow equivalent in complementary terms. At its extreme this idea was developed to the extent of trying, like Seurat, to fragment *all* the colours in terms of the spectrum, building them up with dots and commas of near-primary colours. Greens would be made up of juxtapositions of yellow and blue, violets with blue and red, and so on. This divisionism was not, as so often thought, an essential element of Impressionism, but shows it at the extreme of enthusiasm.

If you look at a sunny landscape in this way, you will find that you can still make a tonal design, but it will not be quite the same sort that you made for your still-life. (In a way full tonality is natural to an interior subject, Impressionism to landscape. Reversed, the methods remain perfectly practicable but become more subjective.) To a much greater extent you can reserve darks for those things which are actually dark in local colour. Cool half-tones may become actually blue or violet, like the full shadows. They need not necessarily be made as dark as nature says they are.

The method of working is therefore very personal, and I can give hints rather than lay down hard and fast rules.

Essentially I think you should start on a white and *not* toned ground, since the colours should remain as fresh and brilliant as possible. Impressionism makes some use of transparent under painting but essentially consists of opaque colours laid side by side; it no longer needs the principle of the warm light-absorbing umber shadow, so there is little point in dulling the intensity of the ground.

Your sense of initial drawing and design should be no less rigorous—do not misunderstand the Impressionists by supposing that they were 'sketchier' than their predecessors; there is usually a lot more work on their canvases.

State the silhouettes of your main objects firmly but lightly on your white canvas. I suggest in some unassertive thin grey or terre verte, which will not interfere with your colour statements.

Now the hard work of comparing colours must be done on the palette, and it is a good idea to decide on a fairly simple colour scheme derived from your subject. I am thinking for the moment in terms of landscape, but this applies to any theme.

While the great Impressionists were not just theorists about colour they did allow the idea of complementary colours to help them in their designs. You will find in very many of their paintings that they chose one main colour (just as in tonal painting) which became the colour theme of the picture, and then used two more principal but slightly subsidiary colours. These other two colours were derived from the other two-thirds of the colour circle. Thus yellow, crimson red, and greenish-blue is a system often found—these are virtually the primaries.

Cézanne all his life dwelt on the theme of orange, green and violet blue—these are the secondary colours. Of course, all sorts of colours entered into his paintings, but he managed to add them up to this simple theme. You will find if you look through even poor colour reproductions of Cézanne that this theme emerges. Sometimes orange plays the dominant role with green and violet blue supporting; sometimes, as in his woodland *sous-bois*, the green naturally predominates.

You will need more colours on your palette for this, but do not multiply them too much. I suggest something like this:

white
lemon or pale cadmium yellow
deep cadmium

cadmium red (or vermilion, but it is *very* expensive)
rose madder
viridian
cobalt blue or French ultramarine
ivory black

To this you might add, as occasion arises, a warmer green such as permanent green (light) and perhaps mineral violet or cobalt violet. Sometimes you will need a sienna or an umber in order to state a rich local brown.

The safe rule is: do not proliferate where you can mix the colour you need. On the other hand do not hesitate to introduce an extra colour if you cannot arrive at it from your existing palette.

To begin, I suggest making a very simple colour sketch before starting on your canvas. It will give you an idea of where your colour should be heading. I sometimes take out small pieces of primed card or offcuts of canvas pinned to a board. You need not make an elaborate drawing, in fact you can block in a virtually abstract equivalent for your landscape—it is the colour notes that you should try to make exact.

Suppose you find like Cézanne (and many other Impressionists) that green supported by orange and blue forms the *main* colour idea. Then, a possible way to start is to mix up something for the brightest green you can see, and put down a blob, quite thickly, in the right place on your canvas. Now on the palette mix up a number of other greens, referring to your subject, until you have a selection of lighter and darker, warmer and cooler green tints. Do *not* mix these by just adding a 'bit of this and that' to some central pile of basic green. Make each colour separately.

When you have a range of four or five different greens, start applying the warmer ones in very simple thin blocks or strokes with large brushes across your canvas. The paint should at this stage be almost transparent, but not so thin that the value of the colour is lost. (It does not matter if some of the turpentine runs to the bottom of the canvas.) The warmer tints go first, because cool values go well on top of warm ones; while warm layers on top of cool layers tend to look heavy and disagreeable.

Gradually you will build up a broad pattern of greens. If you have appreciated the structure of your subject—the planes of the ground, the surfaces and supporting trunks of the trees—this pattern will reflect the fact with a certain sense of order on the canvas. In the course of stating these greens you may find a good deal less of it than you expected; dominant colours often assert themselves optically.

At this stage you may have to restate some of the drawing. Then you may begin looking at the violet greys of the half-tones and shadows. Again, mix up a number of greys (having cleaned off your palette) and start to find their pattern across the subject. Add to this the orange notes and contrasts in a similar way. You will find that you have partly assembled, in broad blocks or wedges, a jigsaw of different values which begin to tell you about the main forms, spaces and recessions of your subject.

There will be a lot of white canvas showing through still. Up to this stage the canvas provides an essential foil to the key and crispness of your values. But you must guard against the danger that these white passages may begin to lend a spurious vitality to your surface. Therefore, when the canvas is surface dry (patience is really an item of equipment in oil painting!) you should begin to obliterate the white, starting from somewhere in the middle and working outwards. Now you will be making statements in more detail, deciding what is more and what is less important to your idea. But you must allow the broad statements of your first layer to control the detail, just as they would in a tonal painting.

One of the great advantages of Impressionism is that it allows an extraordinary flexibility of concentration on the parts of a painting. This does not mean that some parts of a painting can be left simply unstated or uncertain, but it does mean that the explanation of detail can vary very greatly.

I have mentioned Seurat and 'Divisionism'. Seurat carried this to the extreme of 'Pointillism', where the entire surface was made up of dots of pure colour, intermingling to form a logical series of luminous tints. The optical effect did not quite work as Seurat intended—he is a great painter for other reasons—but it is a good exercise for any painter to try once. It eliminates all slickness and facility, and forces a student to consider everything he puts down. Its very tortuousness makes you realise that a good pictorial surface, like a mosaic, is built up of abstract elements, and not from cheat-the-eye passages of illusionism.

The above 'routine' is only a hypothetical way of setting about a subject in Impressionist terms. To the extent that Impressionism was the triumph of personal sensation, so much of course must every painter find his own technique of expression.

Remember though that the Impressionist approach, for all its individualism, did have one important principle which I must again emphasise. It is an escape from the limitations of the dark shadow and the chiaroscuro conventions; this is why it is a release of colour vison. The almost certain road to illusionism and superficiality is the attempt to combine the two conceptions: such attempts are the most blatant hall-mark of flashy Salon painting, which misunderstood the purpose of Impressionism and vulgarised its discoveries. *See illustrations* 3, 16 *and* 29.

(c) Painting in 'saturated' colour: The Fauves

I want to keep 'History of Art' out of this section. But I must refer initially to the post-Impressionists and the Fauves to explain what I mean by 'saturated' colour.

The Impressionists—Monet, Renoir, Sisley and Pissarro were the purest practitioners—raised the key of colour, but did not concern themselves with exploiting all the resulting freedom.

Those of them who began to do so—Van Gogh, Gauguin, Cézanne among them—progressively ceased to be true Impressionists. The opportunity to put down flat slabs of undiluted, 'unshaded' bright colour, almost for the first time since the early Renaissance, was quickly taken up in various ways.

Gauguin took from Emile Bernard the idea of making flat local colours work against each other in space. His Tahitian landscapes and figure paintings are drawn in a mood of symbolism rather than classical modelling—so we find the silhouette outline restored in Gauguin's painting. But he made use of complementary colours, so that his planes stand out in space. This is why the local colours in Gauguin's paintings are so very subjective—orange skies, pink beaches, patterned costumes are made as formal as his outlines. (Sometimes his powers of invention lapsed and he resorted to the commas and blocks of Impressionism in passages of paint quite unsuited to such marks.)

However, largely from Gauguin came the idea that some form of observed painting could be combined with the use of pure colour and saturated tints. A saturated red means, not necessarily the brightest red on the market, but a passage of red which has not had to be broken down or modified for artistic reasons. In tonal painting saturated colours can only be hinted at on the brightest turn of the form; in Impressionism they are modified by atmospheric considerations and the tendency to divide colours into the planes of nature.

What are the motives for painting in flat saturated colour? It is a necessary question to ask oneself. Both tonal and Impressionist painting are a direct response to nature in its illuminated state, however idiosyncratic our own response may be. But the conversion of light into flat patterns of colours is a much more subjective activity.

Gauguin's motives, and those of his group, were complex. He called himself a Synthetist. Partly, he wanted to be a user of symbol in the old sense to express his feelings about people and things in a quasi-religious way. Partly, he felt that the Impressionist 'eye' kept the 'mind' imprisoned. Technically his way out was to paint from the storehouse of memory where particular visual sensations could be transferred into a 'synthesis'—an 'idea'. This was absolutely counter to the scientific principles of Seurat who stood for the ultimate analysis of direct vision. Both attitudes had the slightly self-conscious air of a political stance. Van Gogh, who saw no difference between symbolic meaning and reality, succeeded in integrating his paintings better than either of them.

A revolt from Realism in favour of Symbolism, then, initiated this new feeling for pure colour. There can be other reasons and motives for using colour in this way and I do not want to make too much of an historical aside. Yet if we look at the work of some of the painters who were growing up under the influence of Seurat and Gauguin we can see a surprising development. Bonnard and Vuillard, Matisse, Derain and Marquet, who had all been connected with one camp or the other, found in this new colour freedom the possibility of extending the visual world—not symbolically nor with rigid science, but in a spirit much more akin to that of the Impressionist sensation.

Matisse and the Fauves saw that they might render the bright local colour of nature with the freedom that Monet and Sisley had employed towards atmosphere.

This is a motive which appeals to us all at some time. Here is a gaily coloured fishing boat, a bright flowered dress, a pattern of wallpaper framing a figure in a room—why not express this brilliance and gaiety? Can we do this, and at the same time say something about space and air?

All I have said so far points to obvious difficulties. 'Light excludes colour' —so that we cannot be literal about shadow in a world of bright colours. The Impressionist answer by its nature tends to fragment the colour surfaces in atmospheric terms. The Fauve answer was really an intense simplification of Impressionist colour theory. For a short time they tried simplifying Seurat's Divisionism by using large strokes and dabs of primary and secondary colours laid side by side (see Matisse's *Calme, Luxe et Volupté*) but soon discovered that the 'Simultaneous Contrast' principle could be manipulated with large areas of colour, one tint pushing another back in space. Ultimately it is, like Impressionism, an extension of tonal painting, because Fauve artists insisted that each colour has its 'value' in space. Indeed Matisse as a student in Gustave Moreau's studio produced some beautiful tonal canvases. There is no ambiguity in a Matisse about the order in depth of the colours.

This is achieved in a broad sense by accepting the Impressionist landscape idea that warm colours advance, cool ones retreat. But in Fauve painting a warm crimson is made to 'sit back' by placing notes of a still warmer orange 'in front' of it. To paint in this way, producing the full decorative 'pattern' effect which nature can suggest, is one of the liberties which early Modern painters have given us, and a book such as this must try to help in this direction as much as possible.

The points that I can make are bound to be fragmentary, for while systematic methods of approach almost suggest themselves for tonal painting, the manipulation of bright colour is too subjective and personal to make this possible.

However, you must bear in mind certain things. First, drawing and shape.

74

You will remember that I mentioned Hokusai's skill in avoiding the kind of literal silhouettes which would make the spectator demand literal light and shade. The same problem faced the Fauves (as it had faced Gauguin). It is often said that the literal shapes of photography made artists start formalising and distorting their drawing. I think that it was more the opportunity of using bright colour that caused this.

Clearly the exact representational line that one might expect from academic tradition would be absurd filled up with flat pinks, crimsons and greens. The problem is to find a formalisation of shape appropriate to the kind of reality you can convey.

If we take Matisse as an example (the outstanding example) we can see that a completely flat series of symbols was not enough. His colours might be flat in themselves, but they created a series of planes in depth. His drawing, therefore, while it suggested only a limited amount of individual modelling, had to allow the colour room to move in depth. So we see Matisse using a very simple, though subtle, characterisation of the main shapes in terms of firmly stated outlines, with one or two broad statements about interior modelling serving from the rest. He *must* return to the edge of things in order to accommodate the colour. He distorts these shapes to the extent that the colour is a distortion of visual facts; but the distortions are not random. They have the symbolic content in the simple sense I talked of in the chapter on Drawing— that of making things dramatically recognisable.

But at the same time his edges retain the power of the Contour. One line is still allowed to disappear behind another, and he often leaves gaps to accentuate this, just as Rembrandt did. In this way the individual forms of heads, shawls, bottles, chairs and so on are able to take their place in the limited depth which his colours suggest.

And this is another factor; depth, while it can be conveyed by flat colours, must be limited or it will begin to contradict the sense of pattern which is the essence of such painting.

When I first mentioned colour I pointed out how difficult it is *not* to use colours in depth with our kind of vision. You must be careful that it does not convey too much.

75

My second piece of advice: I think that my precept about not letting too many bright colours compete holds good; indeed in the work of the modern masters I have mentioned it is remarkable how one can find them balancing their colour much as did the Old Masters. Let your painting have some dominant colour; this is more difficult to remember when your work is inclining towards a decorative pattern, but it is the sort of thing in which you can well refer to the modern masters for guidance. Sometimes this can be brought about by a harmony of colours—for instance a 'crescendo' of browns leading through oranges and pinks to one bright scarlet. But often modern painters have used deliberate discords. The major part of a canvas might, in this case, be occupied by blues and greens which would 'clash', except that one note of a bright magenta or scarlet brings them into agreement. This is a sophisticated operation, but do not be disappointed if you produce some unhappy colour contrasts in your early efforts. Contrary to general belief, good colour is just as much a matter of training and experience as any other attribute of art. In fact if you have what is called a 'good taste' for colour do not rely on it alone. Think always of what functions your colour should play in a particular painting, and try to make it 'work' by describing the position of the plane it represents. It sometimes occurs that a particular surface seems to defy any colour that nature suggests. Try simply putting in any tint that 'works in space' in relation to its neighbours, however improbable it seems. You will then very often find, when you look back at your subject, that it was the right one after all.

To what extent are you absolved from thinking about 'tonality' and shadows when you are working with saturated colours?

If you are making something purely symbolic out of flat shapes of colour, in which space plays no part, then the existence of shadow is an intrusion and your work should aspire to harmony rather than tonality of colour.

But if you are translating the visual world, at whatever a decorative remove, then you will find that colour (if it is functioning) will carry an implication of tone. A Matisse conveys a sense of light and shade, just as Rembrandt conveys a sense of local colour. And while Rembrandt will use one note of bright colour (the red of Jan Six's cloak) which suggests the presence of others, so Matisse will sometimes use one cast shadow in a formalised way, so that it stands for all the rest. Like the Impressionists he often makes such shadows no darker than the forms which cast them, simply more blue or more violet.

If you look at Bonnard you will see manipulations of colour which are more closely allied to Impressionism—he contrived to divide his colours far more than Matisse—but you will find transpositions of nature which are just as inventive.

One more point about colour. If you look through colour reproductions of any of the artists I have mentioned, you will get, admittedly a very crude idea of the originals, but you may notice how frequently, even generally, cool colours predominate over warm ones. This seems to be an age-old quality of European painting. I do not think one can lay down any law about this (though Rubens stated that two-thirds of a picture should be of cool tones). It is perhaps an instinctive response to the fact that cool colours predominate in the spectrum, and that seldom more than half of a natural scene is in direct light. Therefore, though I do not claim it as a rule, I think it is a good idea in any sort of painting to let the cool colours control your surface. By this I mean do not put them in as an afterthought, even though they may physically be put down over warm colours. Otherwise they are inclined to become lost in a monotonous grey. It may be an exaggeration to say that bright warm colours will take care of themselves, but you may be sure that the quiet cool ones will not.

The technique of painting with saturated flat colour arises out of tonal painting. Again directness and simplicity of application is the keynote, and again let the work take place on your palette. What goes down on the canvas should be a decision; this is counsel of perfection, but try to maintain it.

Matisse often worked on a pale grey surface. All the same I suggest working from a white ground until you are very sure what will happen. A strongly toned ground generates an assertive 'light and shade' quality as soon as you put a light colour on it.

Pigment should be thick enough to 'cover': transparent passages which do *not* imply shadow can have a weakening dainty effect on a painting, making it look like a water colour. There is no point in massive impastos for their own sake in painting which depends on colour values. Any assertive paint texture simply tends to imprison the subject. It is for this reason that I personally cannot give any advice in the matter of knife painting. To me, almost all paintings done with a knife have a sameness about them, derived from a monotonous similarity of texture. Courbet is an exception—but what a great exception! However, it is a technique so widely used that I cannot suggest you eschew it; I can only plead that it is one of my blind spots.

Remember finally that in this kind of painting as in any other 'directness' does not necessarily mean finishing passages 'all at a go'. It means rather proceeding in an orderly fashion; letting a 'lean' coat of paint dry before you apply a 'fat' one on top of it. Avoid mixing wet paint into a half-dry impasto, or doing the 'mixing' on the canvas. *See illustrations* 20, 30, 35, 36 *and* 39.

(d) Other methods of approach

I have singled out three ways in which representational painting has been approached, technically, in what may broadly be called 'our own times'. The first, from monochrome into tonal values, may be perhaps a 'groundwork' sort of painting nowadays; a valuable introduction to the 'grammar' of painting but not likely to set the Thames on fire.

The new-born visions of Impressionism and the Fauves are of course long since past, but their techniques of painting freshly from a white canvas with calculated values of colour are an inheritance which still serves us well in many directions.

Few later movements have done much to innovate new techniques in oil painting except with the intrusion of new materials.

It is not the purpose of this book to examine in detail other aesthetic schools, because unlike the tonal Realists and Impressionists, they have on the whole made use of existing techniques.

The Cubists, Braque and Picasso in particular, actually returned largely to the tonal build-up of painting for their austere purpose, though they did add to this the idea of collage—the addition of a surface actually stuck on the canvas, usually as a symbol of the subject-matter. The Dada painters extended this with actual objects, but here we enter the world of carpentry.

The German Expressionists probably contributed more to the technique of oil painting as such, than other schools of the century, by making the fiercely

78

moving textures of their pigment play a dominant role in the impact of their paintings. A derivative of this can be seen in England in the work of the Borough Group and its disciples.

The building up of these very thick impastos is sound enough technically if they *are* built up lean to fat. I am less sure of the permanence of thick single layers extended with cement fillers and such like.

New kinds of paint—PVA, acrylic, and the various emulsions on the market have yet to stand the only final test, that of time: but they have been shown to have much value for speed of working, for large mural decorations, and in enlarging to some extent the textural possibilities of painting.

Combinations of material are now so prolific, not only in abstract art but in recent manifestations of figurative painting such as 'Pop', that one cannot hope to codify them. I do not see why any materials should not be used to make a work of art, provided that they serve your purposes. There are two provisos.

First, make sure in your mind that you really have a purpose for them, and are not using them for effect. Secondly, remember that if you sell a painting, you have a responsibility to the buyer in the matter of permanence. Unless you explain frankly that he may be buying an artistic firework, you should try to make your work to last. Whether it does or not is largely a matter of your common sense.

IV Materials

The materials of the artist have been invented and developed in order to let him put his pictorial ideas into practice. This is a truism; yet young painters are often frightened by their materials, a fear which has been aggravated by the phrase 'truth to materials'—invented to suggest that materials possess some inherent aesthetic truth of their own. Perhaps, but the phrase had an origin in the reaction from ornate *trompe l'œil* in the three-dimensional arts. It conveyed simply the healthy idea that one material should not simulate another. A sculptor might carve the likeness of a figure in wood, but he should not thereafter gild it to look like metal; wood has its own quality. I think that this is the best attitude for a painter to take towards his sets of materials. Each artistic idea has its appropriate medium, and to recognise this is the best way to avoid using oil paint to simulate water colour, and so on.

The oil painter is in the happy possession of the most flexible of all the pictorial media; it is as appropriate to the ideas of Braque and Monet as to those of Hals and Fragonard. It remains today the most widely employed material for painting of all kinds, since less than any other medium does it limit an artist's varied powers of expression.

Hundreds of books have been written, wholly or in part, on the subject of the artist's materials; among them there are many which go into the matter with great technical detail, both from the artistic and chemical point of view. Some are admirable; others are admirable in theory, but demand an access to ingredients so difficult to obtain or troublesome to prepare that their recipes are entertaining rather than realistic.

This section has no such pretensions. I want to give only the kind of information which is practical enough for the average student actually to be prepared to implement it. Sometimes the very best possible ways of preparing materials with the highest quality ingredients will, if insisted on, result in his not preparing them at all. My advice is get into the habit of taking trouble with good materials which are readily available and within your means, so that systematic preparation for painting becomes a matter of routine. (You will find that the systematic turns out to be less trouble after all than the makeshift.) You will then be able, at your choice, to investigate the perfectionist recipes given in the authoritative manuals with a much better idea of what you are about. I intend to deal mainly with the materials of oil painting but afterwards I shall give some information about tempera, gouache, water colour and the equipment of the draughtsman; and I shall mention some of the new materials which have come on to the market. Let us take first things first; the subject of 'support', upon which a painting takes place.

Support

If we walk through the galleries of a great collection we notice that canvas seems to make its appearance as a generally used support in the High Renaissance. Most of the so-called 'Primitives' and earlier Renaissance works are on wood panels. Canvas and the development of oil paint seem to have an affinity. This is not entirely for technical reasons; true, the panel is the best support for the kind of ground which receives the tempera media, but it serves oil paint equally well. Canvas has the clear disadvantage of being vulnerable. It can be torn, punctured, dented, stretched and contracted easily by changes in temperature and humidity, and can be rotted by the very paint it supports. But when it comes to large scales, canvas is clearly a winner. It is light, it can be made into a large flat surface easily by stretching, and it can be rolled up for transport. It was the demand for the large 'easel' painting, that is to say 'movable' painting, that gave canvas the popularity it has retained to this day. Added to its convenience canvas has also a texture whose 'tooth' makes it specially sympathetic to the application of oil paint. But it must be remembered that, apart from its texture, canvas is not an inherently superior support, compared to which all others are cheap makeshifts. The use of panels has an even longer history.

Canvas

The best canvas for painting is linen. Cotton and other substitutes are too easily subject to damage (and so, therefore, is the painting on them) because of their elasticity and softness; though, as we shall see, they may be safely used for their textural qualities if they are mounted on panels. I myself find that the softness of cotton makes it technically difficult to work on, but this is only a personal prejudice.

81

Canvas can of course be bought ready primed from the best manufacturers, and except in the matter of price, there is a great deal to be said for this. I think it pays artistically to buy one of the best grades, and, in England, painters are lucky in being able to get the best.

Objections are raised by the experts that artists' colourmen may introduce dryers and amounts of oil into grounds which will allow their products to be quickly sold and long stored, and that these are deleterious to permanence. It may be, but my experience is that the best colourmen can apparently prime canvas better than most others: they are after all, the real experts. But it is true that they cannot provide everyone with exactly the surface he wants, and their primed canvas is very expensive, as any product today must be which still depends on a measure of craftsmanship.

But in talking of grounds I am running a little ahead of myself. Let us take for the moment canvas simply as one of the possible supports for a painting. It is usually possible to buy unprimed canvas (that is, not prepared with a coat of white paint) from artists' colourmen; for small pictures the thinner linen which can be bought in lengths at drapers' stores is quite suitable. It must in all cases be of a tight weave.

STRETCHING A CANVAS

Properly, canvas should receive its priming in lengths and be allowed to mature in this state before it is cut up and stretched in individual pieces. But the amateur will seldom have the space or the equipment for this, and he will do best to fix his raw canvas to the picture stretcher first, and then prime it. A good stretcher consists of four mature lengths of wood slotted at the ends so that they can be fitted together in a way that allows for a slight expansion of the rectangle with wedges. The pieces should be sufficiently wide and solid to prevent warping from humidity, dryness or the pull of the canvas. The cross-section of each piece should display a rounded forward edge on the outside, so that this does not cut into the canvas. From these rounded outer edges, the forward face of the assembled stretcher should slope back to the *inside* edges, so that this face does not make contact with the stretched canvas. Good stretchers are cut in this way in England; on the Continent and in the

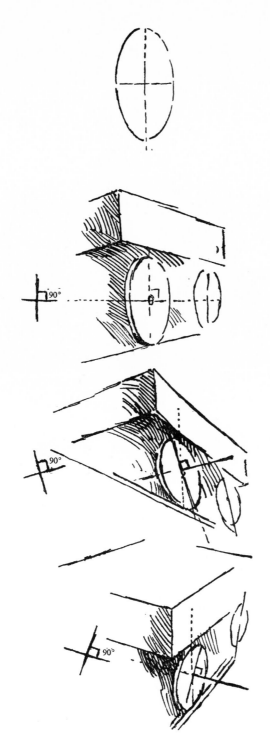

(*See page 113*)

83

U.S.A. it is not always easy to get this quality, but the light-weight square-cut cheap stretcher is a false economy and should be avoided if possible.

To stretch the canvas, cut your pieces to allow about 2 in. all round the stretcher and lay it face down on a table, or on the floor (but the latter will make a very uncomfortable job of it). Fit your stretcher pieces together, making quite sure that all the pieces have the rounded edge facing forwards (see illustration). Knock it firmly together and with a T-square, or by measuring the diagonals with a metal tape, make sure it is quite rectangular. Then place the stretcher rounded edge downwards on the canvas, so that the overlap is equal all round. It should be parallel to the canvas weave. Now tack the canvas to the middle of each of the four sides, driving these four tacks into the narrow outside face of the stretcher. As you do this exert a firm pull, but take care not to distort the rectangle of the stretcher (fig. (a)). Then place pairs of tacks opposite each other working left and right from the middle outwards at intervals of about 2 to $2\frac{1}{2}$ in. until you reach the corners (fig. (b)). Take the corner of the canvas and turn it over the back of the stretcher so that it lies in the junction line of the wood, pointing in, that is, roughly towards the middle of the canvas. Secure with two tacks. You will now have two loops of canvas at each corner (fig. (c)). Fold these over and press down so that the creases join along the junction line of the wood. Again secure with tacks. Tack in the remaining overlap to the back of the canvas, using no more tacks than necessary to hold it in. (You may do this before you tackle the corners if you prefer.) Insert two wedges in each corner so that the right angles of the wedges point outwards and tap these home until the canvas is taut (fig. (d)). It is not necessary to make a drum-surface; the canvas should be taut enough to lie flat and resist light pressure. This is the well-tried classic method of stretching canvas, and is the best way to avoid exasperating folds. If you are fairly 'horny handed' your fingers and thumbs will exert the necessary pull to tense the canvas as you apply the tacks. But a sizeable canvas may leave your fingers quite sore, in which case you should buy a pair of canvas pliers, which are especially made for the purpose.

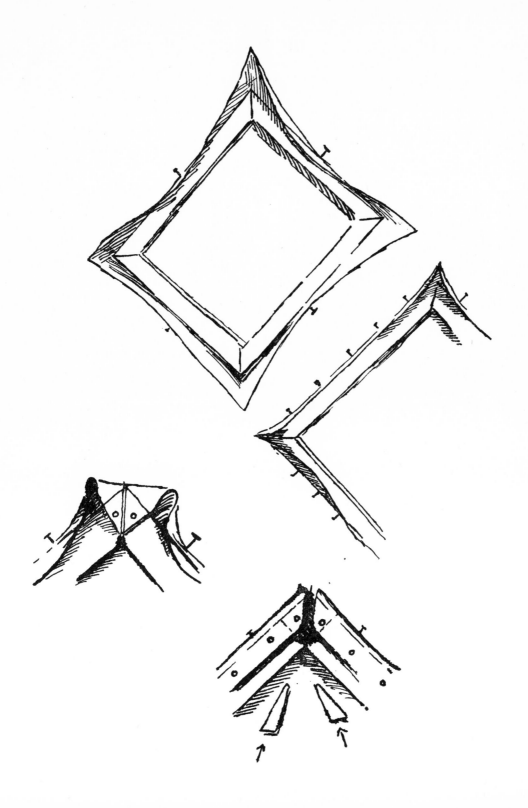

Wood panels

Wood panels are, as I have said, a traditional support for painting. But they must be made of good hard wood, such as oak or mahogany, and well seasoned —that is if you want your painting to last. They should be soaked in warm water to dissolve surface resin and left to dry thoroughly in a warm room. Then if they are not substantially thick in relation to their dimensions, they should be properly cradled.

The disadvantages of the wood panel become apparent in the above short paragraph. They are all very well if you can be sure you have a piece of well-seasoned wood, and if you have the ability in joinery to cradle it properly. The preparation of the surface is no light task. It needs sand-papering, then the application of a good filler, which in its turn must be sand-papered. All this takes a long time and you must be sure your materials are worth it.

Unfortunately there seem to be no ready-made wood panels of this sort on the market. Plywood is sometimes used, but is a dangerous substitute. Modern ply veneers are cut by lathe-like action, and they are really spiral sheets flattened out. The characteristic ripple that often appears in plywood is the attempt of the outer sheets to return to their natural form.

The best panels are probably those you can rescue from reliably aged sources such as old hardwood doors and furniture.

Canvas on panels

The two supports mentioned can be combined. If the fine wood panel, properly prepared, is a thing of the past, a less than perfect piece of wood will still take a facing of canvas. For methods of facing panels or backing canvas see pages 87 and 88 under 'Grounds'.

Card and paper

Both card and paper are traditionally proved supports for oil painting. They must be of good rag manufacture, and this means, alas, that they are likely to become less and less easy to obtain. The difficulty with paper lies in discovering a reliable backing to which it can be glued without distortion. Remember that if you glue paper to card you must do this to both sides of the card to prevent warping.

Hardboard

Hardboard, manufactured in such brands as *Prestwood* and *Masonite*, is a highly compressed pulp sheet bound in resins. It is exceedingly strong, and while it will bend, its various makers claim for it a resistance to distortion and decay which certainly seems borne out by its performance. It is familiar everywhere, as a light building material. Lacking the 'tooth' of canvas, it seems otherwise a technically ideal support for painting. Its ground needs special consideration and will be dealt with below.

Metal

Copper, zinc and aluminium can all be used, and are clearly supports of great strength and permanence. Painters have worried that paint may tend to flake off such a very hard non-absorbent surface, but this is not borne out by seventeenth-century paintings on copper. Weight, expense, and the difficulty of cutting are points against metal supports. In their favour they seem to be permanent and less liable to shrinkage or expansion than anything except hardboard. They need only sand-papering as a ground.

Grounds

The 'ground' is the pigment with which the surface of a support is prepared before painting. First, without a ground the support may be chemically injured by the oil of the paint. Secondly, the support (unless it is a metal) will almost certainly be absorbent and will obstruct the process of painting. Thirdly, oil paint tends to darken and 'saponify' or become transparent, and this can be countered by an underlying ground (provided, of course, that it is white).

Canvas

Canvas is both vulnerable and absorbent. It should therefore always have a ground applied to it. This is done in two stages—sizing and priming. Size is a glue of some form, and this coat is necessary to protect the canvas from the priming that follows if it is an oil priming, and in any case to render the surface and the weave non-absorbent.

Sizing is a matter of experience. The purists may say that you must melt down genuine parchment or rabbit skin, and you can find recipes for this. But most of us have hardly the time for a fundamentalist approach to all our materials. A good quality joiner's glue or size crystal, or a good proprietary glue will do very well. The difficulty is to dissolve it to the right consistency. Glue should be melted in hot water. About $\frac{1}{2}$ lb. of sheet glue to $1\frac{1}{2}$ pts. of water will produce a liquid which may be a little on the thin side, depending on the glue. The water content can be reduced if necessary by further 'cooking'. (Carpenters' glue is traditionally prepared in a double boiler or size-pot.) The size when warm should not be sticky like syrup, but should run from the brush in a creamy flow. When cold it should be a wobbly, easily broken jelly.

The size can be applied in its cold jelly form to the canvas with a squeegee, but this is a professional process.

If you size the canvas on a stretcher, it must not be wedged taut first or its shrinking will distort the stretcher. It must be just loose enough to take up the right tension when sized and this is a matter of practice.

Apply the size warm but not hot with a large house-painter's brush, so that it goes on like a rich water wash, quickly and cleanly. If it starts forming lumps and ridges, or offers a sticky resistance to the brush, it is too thick or too cold. It should not form a gluey skin on top of the canvas, but when dry should be seen to have imparted a sheen to the texture. I emphasise that you must not make a crackable sheet of glue on the surface; the size is there simply to interpose itself between canvas and priming. Some painters apply two coats, but one coat just right is enough. Over-thickness will be evident; over-thinness of glue will reveal itself, if, upon priming, beads of white paint or oil stains appear on the back of the canvas.

The next stage is the priming, over which no two experts seem to agree. If a surface is rigid it is fairly easy to make a priming obey the painting rule of 'start lean, end fat'. That is, it need have very little oil in it. But canvas is flexible, and so the priming must be supple enough not to crack. A good oil priming will have enough oil to prevent this, but not enough to give a shiny skin of oil to the surface. Of course, the more oil the more the tendency of the priming is to darken.

The house-painter's method is good basic practice. A builder's undercoat for white paint will itself be an oil paint, but low in oil and without varnish content. When thinned to the right degree with turpentine it will dry matt, even semi-transparent. A thorough house-painter will apply two or more undercoats before he proceeds to the layers of top paint.

So it should be with canvas. Whatever the media and pigments of your priming, do not apply one thick coat. It may crack, and will amost certainly dry (when it does eventually dry) in shiny unpleasant ridges of oil. A first coat should be rubbed in—if necessary thinned somewhat with turpentine—so that it does no more than fill the crevices of the canvas. It should barely 'cover'— that is to say it should retain an element of transparency and will be grey rather than white. The exact degree of cover a first coat gives depends, though, on the pigments used. The second coat should be enough to cover the surface with an opaque white, but again should be 'lean' and thus enough not to build up an impasto. It should not, of course, be applied until the first is dry. When this second coat is dry, a third will do no harm; but again it must not start to form solid ridges and lumps. I usually rub rather than brush each coat on, sweeping any surplus off with a palette knife.

White lead is not the only oil priming for canvas though it is probably the most widely used.

You can buy good oil priming paint from any good artists' colourmen; or you can buy builders' undercoat. But there is a difficulty here. Now that various kinds of plastic emulsions are so generally used, the undercoats have naturally followed suit. It is not easy to buy a genuine white lead undercoat of the sort which is suitable, but you should make sure that this is what you are getting. *Nine Elms* genuine white undercoat is a reliable brand, and it is worth finding the local paint shops or ironmongers which sell it. I advise against the practice of making undercoat from dry white lead, because it is extremely poisonous, and can be breathed when in its powdered state. *Stack white* can be bought at paint merchants. This is white lead made in a particular way and ground in oil: it is much safer to use. But it is often lumpy and difficult to prepare; messing about with white lead can have a bad effect on the skin. So leave it to experts, or get an experienced craftsman to give you a practical demonstration.

There are alternative grounds to white lead. A traditional pigment is zinc oxide. This is safe to use and is a pure white. However, it has a tendency to crack, and dries more slowly than white lead. It is probably less suitable for canvas, though as a constituent in a ground for panels it is excellent.

Titanium white, which has been in use for some decades, is claimed as the answer to the disadvantages of lead and zinc. Everything suggests that it is inert and permanent in association with other colours, and incidentally it is not poisonous. It is very dense, and can be bought as an undercoat ready prepared for priming from artists' colourmen. I have found that a ground of titanium has a tendency to glossiness when dry, which can be reduced by rubbing with pumice.

Whether you use white lead, zinc or titanium, or mixtures of any two of them, the ground should be applied as I have described.

If you want to be thorough, you should protect the back of your canvas from atmospheric moisture and dirt. There are numerous recipes for this, from which I select a coat of wax varnish as simple and efficient. But you cannot apply this after the canvas is stretched: so you must go to the trouble of un-stretching your primed canvas and lightly restretching it in reverse, when the back can then be varnished. Then of course you must again go through the process of reversing and restretching. I have to admit that for most painters the usual alternative is to do nothing; but rather than this at least glue a piece of tough brown paper across the back of the stretcher (not to the canvas).

Marouflage
Marouflage is the process of sticking a canvas to a panel. This protects the

canvas from both damage and atmospheric change. Seasoned wood panelling, or a strong builder's board such as chip-board, will serve as a support. If hardboard is used it should be 'marouflaged' on both sides except for small pictures, otherwise the whole surface may be pulled into a curve during drying.

To marouflage a canvas the adhesive should have a varnish base. Hilaire Hiler in his *Notes on the Technique of Painting* gives:

Venice turpentine—1 part
oil copal varnish (commercial)—1 part
Add—white lead powder (with the aforesaid poison warning) until a putty is formed which is too thick to spread with a brush, but which can be spread evenly with a palette knife.

This putty should be spread thickly and evenly on the support. The canvas (priming upwards!) is then unrolled onto the panel leaving a margin of canvas. It should then be pressed from the middle outwards with a soft pad or a small lino-cutter's roller. The margin can then be cut off—when the panel is dry.

Panels

The process of sizing and priming wood and card panels is the same in principle as that for canvas. It may be found that panels need two coats of size if the first is heavily absorbed, but the same precautions about thickness should be observed.

When, however, we come to the composition of the white ground for a panel, we can pick and choose as we cannot with canvas. A panel is, or should be, rigid; so there is not the same necessity here for flexibility in a ground.

There are many recipes for panel grounds suitable for oil painting. Here are some basic ones:

Oil ground
(1) white lead undercoat as for canvas (v. sup.)
(2) zinc oxide powder ⎫
 white lead powder ⎬ equal parts
 linseed oil ⎭
The powder should be well mingled and the oil worked in with a palette

knife on a sheet of glass until it becomes a paint which can be worked somewhat dryly with a brush. It can then be thinned with turpentine.

(3) zinc oxide powder—5 or 6 parts
    whiting—1 part
    linseed oil—equal parts

Half oil ground
    zinc oxide powder—5 parts
    chalk powder—$\frac{1}{2}$ part
    size—1 part
    boiled linseed oil—1 part
    water—5 parts
These amounts refer to volume.

Mix water and size until amalgamated. Then mix in zinc oxide and chalk until smooth. Drip in the oil slowly, stirring all the time. The water throughout this process should be warm but not boiling. When cold the mixture may jellify in which case it should be warmed for application to the surface.

Hardboard

Dark hardboard such as *Prestwood* or *Masonite* is an exception to the rule of sizing. Such board should *not* be glue-sized. This is because its binding agent has a high water-resistant content; in fact salvaged cargoes of hardboard have survived immersion in sea water.

The above half-oil priming, applied direct, seems perfectly adhesive, and has to my knowledge stood the test of a decade. At least three coats are needed for a satisfactory surface, and they should be applied to the *smooth* side of the board, not the textured side. This smooth surface should be finely sand-papered before priming.

This half-oil priming has the advantage of rapid drying. In a warm room, two coats may be applied in one day, the third on the next day. Leave one more day and it is ready for painting. Again resist the temptation to apply one thick coat. The first coat should be rubbed in, the next two brushed across at right angles to one another. The result may be sand-papered lightly.

This priming makes an attractive working surface. Its slight absorbency may be reduced by the addition of a little more oil to your turpentine in the first painting.

Glue grounds

On really firm panels (except hardboard) glue grounds may be used. They eliminate the tendency of oil to darken, and in themselves these grounds preserve a strong whiteness. But on the other hand they immediately absorb oil from the paint laid on them and I think their advantage for oil painting is dubious.

They should be used only by those who want a really absorbent ground, or who wish to conduct an underpainting in egg tempera.

1. zinc white powder
   whiting
   glue size
   (This is the half-oil priming without the oil; the oil content may be simply reduced rather than omitted.)
2. whiting
   glue
   cold milk
   Make a size with equal parts of milk and water. Add whiting until a medium cream results. Apply hot.

Since oil absorption will occur on these grounds, I advise the addition of at least a little oil in the first place to form an emulsion.

A pure glue ground can be strengthened by the laying of an unprimed linen (not necessarily of fine weave) into the first coat. A further coat or coats may then be worked into the cloth with a knife, so that the cloth and glue priming forms virtually one mass. An overlap of cloth should be turned round and stuck to the back after the front surface is dry.

If this is done the first coat of glue priming should be thick enough to enter the weave and act as a thorough adhesive. It is a form of marouflage and is an attractive painting surface.

Gesso

'Gesso' is a word used so loosely that in various manuals it is taken to mean almost any sort of priming. Its use should denote the existence of glue as an element in the binder, as in the examples above; it is the name given to the particular plaster of Paris ground used for tempera painting, and (with variations) for the preparation of frames and painted furniture.

The preparation of gesso panels for tempera painting is a lengthy business, and beyond my present scope. Good recipes and procedures may be found in manuals such as Doerner and Hiler. Rowney's produce ready prepared egg tempera panels.

Summing up

It is good practice to prepare your own grounds at least sometimes, for it teaches you as nothing else can the physical nature of painting from top to bottom.

If you want the fullest range of resonant dark tones, then use non-absorbent oil primings, remembering that these will tend to lessen in brilliance. Reserve absorbent grounds for paintings of high key.

Remember that a painting is, at best, as permanent as the surface it is done on: there is no point in using fine pigments on cheap cardboard, pieces of packing case, or inferior cloth.

Remember finally that the more oil the longer the drying time. So do not wait until you need a painting surface. Prepare a number of panels and canvases; then put them away for a month or two. If in this time they yellow, exposure to natural light for a few days before use should restore their whiteness.

Pigments

Pigments for paint are made of a variety of substances, some permanent, others fugitive. Some which suit one medium do not suit another.

In former times painters ground their own colours and mixed them with the required medium as needed, most pigments being reducible to a powder. Few artists do this now, as colourmen do it for them. The best colourmen list the colours which they consider permanent, those which may be fugitive in certain mixtures, and those for which they make no claim. Their permanent colours are very reliable and their main disadvantage is that they are ground and mixed for general sale, not to suit the individual. This means that their tubes have a lot of oil to lengthen their 'shelf life' in the shops; this can be extracted very simply on blotting paper or newspaper. They are also ground very finely so that their texture sometimes lacks the body of a home-ground mixture. A number of books will tell you how to grind your own pigments if you want to, but it is a long business and you are likely to find yourself doing nothing else. It is really better to leave such activities until you really know the finer points of what you want. Learn to paint first, and be glad that others have taken some of the work off your hands.

This is a short list of well-tried permanent or semi-permanent oil colours which will cover most of your needs.

Whites

Flake white—This is the usual trade name for white lead. Sometimes called *cremnitz white* or *silver white* when ground in oil, it is very strong and resists cracking; it has a good body: that is to say it will make a good impasto. Disadvantages: very poisonous and affects some colours, notably rose madder and French ultramarine, perhaps the cadmiums.

Zinc white—Considered unsatisfactory in oil. An intense white, but liable to crack and is a slower drier.

Titanium white—Claimed as the answer to the disadvantages of lead and zinc. Chemically inert, it does not affect other pigments, appears not to crack or darken and has an excellent cover. It lacks the body of flake white, and at least in some of the examples I have used tends to encourage an oily skin, but this may simply be due to an excess of oil in the manufacture, which can be soaked off on paper before use.

Because of its density it seems to need a lot of colour to saturate it, so that a little goes a long way in lightening other pigments. If you are used to flake white, titanium needs some adjusting to on the palette.

Yellows

Lemon yellow—Now chemically prepared. A pure pale yellow with a tint of green. A particularly characteristic lemon yellow is produced by Robersons.

Cadmium yellow—Usually produced in two additional hues, *pale* and *deep*. Must be the best artists' colours, in which case they are permanent. Never use with emerald green or Naples yellow.

Chrome yellow—Chromate of lead. Considered less permanent than the cadmiums, and does not add greatly to the palette.

Yellow ochre—A natural ferric hydrate pigment. A very safe permanent colour and basic to most palettes. It is opaque and may be mixed with any other colours. Varies in hue; other varieties are *brown ochre* and *golden ochre*.

Raw sienna—A variety of ochre not unlike golden ochre. Permanent but takes up a lot of oil, so is a bad drier.

Naples yellow—There is an original Naples yellow which is now usually imitated with mixtures of other yellows and white. As you can easily do this yourself it is not an essential colour, though widely popular.

Indian yellow—Unobtainable in genuine form, but a chemical substitute is claimed as sound. Not essential, but produces a very brilliant transparent orange gold hue which cannot quite be simulated, so occasionally useful. I have found it a slow drier.

Reds

Cadmiums—Under *orange*, *red*, *scarlet* this range provides the most reliable of reds. Cadmium orange might be grouped under yellows but becomes pinker when mixed with white.

Vermilion—A beautiful red which cannot quite be simulated by mixtures, but it is very expensive and perhaps less permanent than cadmium. Not necessary, a luxury.

Rose madder—A beautiful blue crimson made from a root. Often simulated by alizarin dyes, but a genuine rose madder is put out by Rowney's on their permanent list. Said to be fugitive in thin glazes and attacked by white lead.

Alizarin crimson—Cheaper than rose madder, but lacks its subtlety. May

96

crack in thin glazes. It is a synthetic colour with a very strong staining power and is apt to swamp the palette. Use with reserve.

Indian red—Red oxide. A very heavy opaque bluish-red. Permanent and useful, but very powerful. Easily swamps other colours.

Light red—Burnt ochre. A very good basic brown-red. Permanent.

Venetian red—Somewhat between light red and Indian red in hue. Very powerful; can swamp the palette. Permanent.

Blues

Cobalt blue—Cobalt aluminate. A basic 'primary' blue, permanent and perhaps the most useful of blues.

Cerulean blue—A different form of cobalt. Expensive, but very bright and a pure greenish-blue. Its name should not lead one to assume that it is the happiest colour for skies. Not essential, but useful.

Prussian blue—The best is said to be permanent, but it has acquired a bad reputation as a fugitive hue. It is perhaps the most notorious of palette swampers. I think it best avoided by the inexperienced.

French ultramarine (French blue)—A brilliant purplish 'royal blue'. A much used and indeed useful colour, but I have taken to doing without it. It has a rather disagreeable stringy texture even when extended by other colours and is attacked by flake white. It is claimed as permanent as long as it is not attacked by acids. However, there is no close substitute except—

Genuine ultramarine—for which French blue is itself the substitute. This is one of the oldest of blues and is perhaps the most pure and lovely of all pigments. As it is ground lapis lazuli, it is almost prohibitively expensive, and it is for this reason I mention it rather than recommend it.

Monastral blue—An artificial dye colour, claimed as permanent. It is very strong transparent greenish-blue, and may be used as a base for mixing a substitute for the suspect Prussian blue. Winsor and Newton produce this as Winsor blue.

Greens

Do not buy a lot of tubes of secondary colours which are mixtures of what you already have.

Viridian—Almost the one really necessary green. It is a very permanent pure cold green which produces brilliant warm colours combined with lemon or cadmium yellow. It is also useful in adjusting cobalt towards a greener blue. Also sold as *emerald oxide of chromium*. As '*vert émeraude*' it must not be confused with—

Emerald green—A very brilliant 'exact' green and extremely poisonous. Avoid it for this reason alone, though it is in fact affected by a number of other colours. A safe substitute is on the market but be sure you are getting it.

Permanent green light—A mixture of viridian and zinc yellow. Not necessary, but useful if you need an immediate bright green of dense body. Make sure it comes from the selected list of a good colourman.

Terre verte—Should be a natural earth; though sometimes nowadays tickled up with viridian which spoils its quality. A very delicate transparent earthy green; most useful as a preliminary colour for drawing in, as it does little to disturb subsequent colours. Is, incidentally, the traditional underpainting for tempera.

Browns, blacks and violets

Raw umber—A natural pigment. A basic colour for underpainting, though it can have a gloomy effect if such work is continued in this colour too far. Has therefore a reputation as a somewhat 'old-fashioned' colour. Permanent. A good drier.

Burnt umber—Calcined raw umber. A rich deep transparent brown. Permanent. Both these colours vary with the variation in the actual source mineral.

Burnt sienna—Calcined raw sienna. A brilliant reddish-brown. Permanent.

Ivory black—Permanent. Perhaps the most widely used black. A slow drier.

Lamp black—Permanent and slightly warmer in mixtures than ivory black.

Cobalt violet—A pure violet of various shades. Permanent, except in conjunction with white lead or a metal palette knife.

Mars violet—Iron oxide. Permanent and very solid in body. All the other mars colours—yellow, brown, red, orange—are permanent.

The above is a very brief selection of colours from the large range which the trade publishes. You will find numbers of alternatives on the 'permanent' lists, but remember that you do not need as many colours as I have mentioned to paint a picture.

The drying powers of some oil pigments

Fast
Flake white
Aureolin
Burnt sienna
Raw umber
Burnt umber

Medium
Cobalt green
Cobalt blue
Cobalt violet
Indian red
The mars colours
Viridian

Slow
Terre verte
Cerulean
French ultramarine
Yellow ochre
Cadmium red
Cadmium orange
Ivory black
Zinc white
Vermilion

For permanence it is wise to choose your colours within the two top categories issued by such reputable colourmen as Winsor and Newton, Roberson and Rowney.

Media

A medium is the liquid in which a pigment is ground in order to make it workable and adhere to the ground.

In oil paintings the characteristic of the medium is that it solidifies, whereas in water colour the bulk of it evaporates, leaving a soluble or semi-soluble gum.

A large number of oils have been used or at least tried as vehicles for painting. Of these the two most successful are linseed oil and poppy oil; nut oils and the like need not concern us here in this résumé.

Since oils have a tendency to form a surface skin, drying by oxidation, it is necessary when paint is to be worked loosely and thinly to add a thinning agent. The most successful have been found to be turpentine and petrol. It must be remembered that these thinners have no quality as binding agents, and indeed perform a function not dissimilar to that of water in water colour painting— that is, they evaporate when their job is done. They are used simply because the necessary thin flow of paint needed at some stages could otherwise only be obtained by an excess of oil. An underpainting, for instance, would form a wrinkling, slow-drying skin, which exactly contradicts the principle 'start lean, end fat'. But students are apt to assume that turpentine is a medium itself, forgetting that the oil in the tube is doing this job. Both turpentine and petrol are solvents; in excess they may dissolve the oil to such an extent as to leave the pigment in semi-powder form on the canvas.

Linseed oil

This is, as its name implies, a vegetable oil extracted from the seed and purified by various methods. It contains chemicals which make it very tough and permanent when dry. Its process of drying is complex, consisting not of evaporation but of a chemical exchange in contact with the air. It is further complicated by the fact that some pigments hasten this process more than others— an argument in favour of thorough amalgamation during the mixing of different colours on the palette.

Linseed oil tends to darken, but only up to a point. Traditionally this tendency is agreed to be arrested by ordinary daylight. It is the most reliable and strongest of the painting vehicles, and as long as the best available quality is bought there is no need to look for another.

Poppy oil

This is said to have been much used by French painters in the nineteenth century. It is usually lighter in appearance than linseed but may eventually darken more. It is a slower dryer and more porous. For these reasons it is not so much used nowadays as a painting oil; but it is often used to grind pigments, as its slower drying keeps paint workable for longer in the tube.

There is no advantage in using it to paint with where linseed is available. It need only be added that the two oils are much alike chemically so that there seems no harm in extending with linseed what may be poppy oil in tube.

Boiled oil

Boiled linseed oil or 'stand oil' is prepared for its special qualities of durability and is used by coach painters. It has the disadvantage for most painters of being a slow dryer.

Turpentine

Essence or spirits of turpentine is a distilled resin spirit, and is the most commonly used thinner for painting. 'Turpentine substitute' is no substitute for the painter, and I do not advise it even for washing brushes.

Turpentine must be of good quality; artists' colourmen produce this, but rather expensively. It can be got from a chemist, not always easily; or from an ironmongers—both more cheaply. Test an ironmonger's product by dropping some on white blotting paper. It should dry without leaving a stain. Buy small quantities, or transfer the contents of a large bottle to full, tightly corked small ones, since turpentine in air becomes resinous, even in bottle, and then does not dry. The old custom was to top up flagons of turpentine with glass marbles in order to exclude air. It is supposed to be kept away from the light.

Petrol

This is claimed as an even better thinner than turpentine as it evaporates completely. I think it is technically quite sound, though it is such a powerful solvent that it tends to make paint matt and dead; but this is really a matter of exercising great care with its proportions to oil. Disadvantages are its rapid evaporation which can be a nuisance on the palette; a stock of raw petrol about the house is an obvious fire hazard; and the smell of petrol often puts people off—including myself.

Varnishes

Varnishes are fast-drying resins dissolved in oil or spirits. They have been used not only as 'protective skins' over finished pictures, but as actual painters' media. They aid the drying of oils and help to maintain the brilliance of the colours. Used alone they are very tricky, leading to shiny and cracking surfaces; and of course a painting so carried out is at the mercy of any cleaner who in ignorance sets about removing a top varnish. *Copal*, *Mastic* and *Damar* are varnishes commonly incorporated in oil and turpentine to form a compound medium. Copal is very hard when dry, but may cause cracks if its strength is not matched by the ground under it. 'Double Mastic', the form of mastic incorporated in a painting medium, will bring up the colours to their full depth; it is apt to cause a shiny surface if only a little too much is used. I person-ally use Damar, when I include varnish at all in my medium, since it seems to enrich the colours without causing the shine and harshness of the others. Authorities vary so greatly about the identity and proportions of media used by the Masters and in their suggestions for present practice that I can offer no cut and dried formula. But here is a suggestion:

> Damar   not more than 1 part
> Linseed oil   not more than 2 parts
> Turpentine according to the layer of paint
> (Remember always—start lean, end fat)

There is perhaps not much virtue in varnish as an element in light-keyed paintings; its use lies in sustaining the resonance of the darker, and usually underlying tones. These are the surfaces which can easily sink and 'go dead' when thinned with pure turpentine. On the other hand, shadow areas fail in their purpose if they reflect light instead of absorbing it; the oil-varnish content of such passages should be enough to keep the paint 'up', not enough to make it shine. It is really a matter of personal experience and common sense.

Brushes

Hogs

The oil painter may be well advised to start by using hog-bristle brushes. The sable brush, which is similar in feel and strength to a good water colour brush, is useful for small details and fine lines, but it can easily encourage weak imitative statements. It is the 'hog' which can carry a body of paint and transfer it squarely to the canvas without a saturation of liquid. With it the painter is forced to put down values of colour side by side where the sable leads to a 'slithery' fusing of brush marks.

Hog brushes are usually sold as long round, long, and short square or flat, and filbert. The last is a flattened head of bristles which narrows to a point.

The long round is by far the most versatile type of hog brush, and I advise this in several sizes as basic equipment. Long flats are handy, though not essential, for some passages; I have never found a use for short flats.

Filberts can be useful, according to taste, but they must be properly made, and this means that the bristles should be so selected and assembled that their natural curves take up the 'filbert' shape. This is also true, ideally of long rounds. Filberts which are really square brushes trimmed with a knife to look like filberts should be avoided, as should obviously trimmed round brushes. They will certainly take on very quickly a splayed shape which makes precise painting almost an impossibility. In fact any cheap quality brush will tend to splay. Of all your materials do not economise on brushes, but buy the best. It is better to have six good brushes than sixty bad ones. Remember also that it is not washing but lack of washing that wears out a brush.

Sables

Again, do not economise. After some experience, you may find that you are the exception who really paints better with sables. In this case, buy a good range of sizes. Otherwise, in conjunction with hogs, two or three should be enough and they should be small, since this is the point of having them.

Knives

A palette knife is essential equipment, and should be the instrument with which pigments are mixed on the palette. The straight variety is the most practical for this purpose. I prefer quite a small knife; it does its job quite as effectively as a large one and is less tiring to use.

The trowel shaped kind of knife is properly speaking a painting knife. If you want to paint with a knife, this is the kind to use. I suggest one with a short, triangular blade, which should have good flexibility.

If you forget to wipe your knife clean and a coat of dry paint forms on it, do not *burn* it clean (a common practice), as this rapidly weakens the metal. Either sand-paper it off or use paint remover.

Easels

For indoor work on canvas up to four or five feet in width, the standard art school 'radial' type easel is perfectly stable and very convenient. It is easy to move, it tips forward and can be adjusted to most heights needed. I personally have found them more stable than some of the lighter 'studio' easels. 'Studio' easels are the type consisting of a framework carried on a four-wheeled base. A really well-made large studio easel is an extremely expensive piece of furniture, all right if you have a permanent studio and can afford it. Otherwise, the 'radial' easel is adequate, and has the inherent advantage of being borne on three legs, not four, so that it does not need to be adjusted to an irregular floor. A very large canvas can be held on two such easels.

Sketching easels

The conflict between weight and stability makes the choice of a sketching easel difficult. It is essential to have an easel providing some means of tipping the canvas forward.

104

The cheapest practical easel is produced in very similar pattern by several firms. It consists of three adjustable-height legs meeting in an apex joint. Through this joint slides an upright arm which can be raised and tipped forward. The canvas is held between the top of this arm and blocks on the two forward legs.

With a little trouble the stability of any sketching easel can be increased by guying it out with three lengths of picture cord secured on the ground by metal skewers. These can easily be carried in the paint-box and will allow you to defy quite strong breezes.

Another well-tried type is the paint-box and easel combined. This is a box with three legs which extend to a wide tripod. On the top is the easel itself, a frame which is lifted and has an adjustable upright. It will carry canvases up to 30 in. high. These are expensive, but have the advantages that the weight of the paints themselves acts to stabilise the easel, and you have a convenient table top behind the canvas for putting bottles on. The paints are held in a drawer which pulls forward. It is heavy but self-contained. Everything, paints, media, palette and canvas, is carried by one handle.

There are other elaborate collapsible easels with built-in stools and dipper holders. But I advise simplicity: if you want to sit, buy a comfortable camp stool which weighs almost nothing and can easily be strapped to your box.

Palettes

Many painters prefer a fixed palette to one held in the hand. If you have a table to one side of your easel, or better still a small stand just in front of it, you can use any smooth agreeable surface as a palette. A sheet of glass with a neutral coloured paper under it does very well. A panel of hardboard, if wiped clean after use, soon acquires a pleasant mature surface.

Hand palettes

The main requirement is that they should not be too heavy. They can be rectangular or 'kidney-shaped' to taste: the thumb hole should be big enough and close enough to the edge not to tire the hand. If a new palette is varnished, sand-paper it down finely to the wood on the working side. A new palette will absorb oil, but with a few days of use it will begin to mature.

ARRANGEMENT OF THE PALETTE

Place your paints round the palette systematically. It is usual to have the white nearest the hand and to place outwards round the further edge successively the yellows, reds, greens, blues, earth colours and blacks. Squeeze out rather more than you think you will need. If you are leaving your palette unused for some period, the surplus paint can be placed with the knife in a shallow tray and covered with water. But remember to let the water dry off before working again!

Dippers

Clip-on dippers can be bought very cheaply. They should be the kind with a removable rim which allows them to be thoroughly cleaned out, since residues of old sticky medium are strictly to be avoided. For a fixed palette, many painters prefer to keep a stock of empty jam jars and tins, to be used and thrown away.

Other items

In addition to the specific materials of painting, every painter should keep about him plenty of rag, sheets of newspaper, string, drawing pins, a hammer and screwdriver, a corkscrew, tin tacks and any other apparently trivial things whose lack is not noticed until the last moment. Also he should keep a stock of drawing paper and pencils for any notes and ideas he may need to jot down while painting. Nothing is more irritating than to be held up for want of a box of tacks or a piece of rag.

Drawing materials and water colours

It is not my concern to deal with the materials of water colour in detail. But the oil painter will need an adequate equipment at hand for the matter of preparing notes. The following is a short list of the essentials, which the painter may extend at choice.

Drawing

> pencils—A supply of good quality pencils from HB to 4B. Always keep some short pencils in your pocket for notes.
>
> penknife
>
> conté and chalk pencils
>
> a packet of vine charcoal
>
> a cheap fixative spray and a bottle of fixative
>
> a drawing pen (*not* a mapping pen)—an ordinary cheap pen-holder with a stock of large pointed school nibs, not too fine. Avoid ball pointed nibs, etc.
>
> drawing inks—Indian ink is inflexibly black. Better for general purposes a good sepia. Do not use a soluble ink if you are going to add a wash.

Paper and support

A heavy good quality cartridge with a matt surface will serve most purposes. Expensive water colour and tinted papers of good rag quality are of course excellent technically, but their expense is apt to inhibit the painter whose job is that of making notes and studies. A light half-imperial drawing board and a stock of good drawing pins are indispensable.

Water colours

> colour box—A medium sized box with holders for about eight or ten artists' quality half-pans, and double palette. Thumb rings on the base.
>
> colours—Keep these to a minimum. Here is a selected list:
>> chinese white
>>
>> aurora or lemon yellow
>>
>> yellow ochre
>>
>> light red

vermilion
cobalt blue
cyanine blue
viridian
burnt sienna
ivory black

For brief statements about warm and cool tones, with reminders of local colour supported by written notes the following will be enough:

chinese white
yellow ochre
light red
cobalt blue
ivory black

Brushes—One medium sized camel or sable hair brush will do everything you need from generous washes to pencil lines. You must make quite sure it comes to a fine point, and reputable artists' shops will wash out any filling and test this for you in a glass of water at the counter.

Other equipment:
an aluminium camp chair, with a back, not arms
a good supply of water (rain water is best)
rag
a tin for water
a ruler
drawing books—Ring-backed books of good cartridge are convenient. But remember to fix your drawings or they will rub. And do not be bullied by the format: rule off your working space to the proportion you need. Avoid blocks of paper, which always crackle under washes of colour.
erasers—A soft rubber—but I incline to the traditional advice that you should try and do without.

Recent colour innovations

Tempera

This is of course among the most ancient of media. For some years Rowney's have put on the market a genuine egg tempera in tubes which can be used on its own or as an underpainting for oils. Their lists should be referred to for the colours available.

Plastic colour

Plastic paints with acrylic and polymer bases have recently been put on the market for the use of artists. They have a good cover and dry matt and quickly; they have already been used to good effect in large abstract and mural paintings. They lack the body and flexibility of oil paint and their quality of permanence has yet to stand the test of time.

V Perspective

The natural place for this subject, it may be thought, is along with design and drawing. And of course it belongs there. But I am most anxious to associate design and drawing as closely as possible in the reader's mind with colour; and nothing can prove such a barrier to this as the wrong sort of preoccupation with perspective. This is commonly regarded as an additional implement in the hands of the artist. It is—in the sense that organised systems of perspective have been evolved. But in another sense *any* representation of solid nature on a flat surface is in perspective, whether the artist likes it or not. If he does not like it, then the kind of perspective that goes into his painting will probably be random instead of systematic, but it will exist.

I have said that every straight line in nature can be seen as having a 'bearing', as if it were a compass needle or a clock hand pointing in some one direction. It would seem that it is only necessary to estimate these bearings accurately with a straight-edge held out before one's eye, repeat them on the drawing paper or canvas, and the linear part of the work will be 'in perspective'. Thus nature's lines-in-depth would be projected accurately onto a flat surface and we would have on our surface a one-eyed version of what we see.

But unfortunately, while we paint and draw on a flat surface, we do not see on a flat surface. As you look from one point to another, imagine a series of straight lines radiating out from your eye to each successive point. Now suppose yourself to be tracing nature through some transparent surface. If the surface you were drawing on were at right angles to every one of those radiating lines it would be the concave inner surface of a sphere. This is the only surface you can project depth onto with linear accuracy. But like the map maker you are in the difficulty that while you can roll a piece of paper or canvas into a cylinder or a cone, you cannot make it spherical. You cannot help distorting the facts to some degree; perspective systems, like map projections, are forms of organised distortion.

This is why I say that *any* form of representing depth on a flat surface is 'perspective' in that it must be a departure from the directions you actually see. Some sort of instinctive perspective is built into the act of representing depth (though not into the act of making flat symbols).

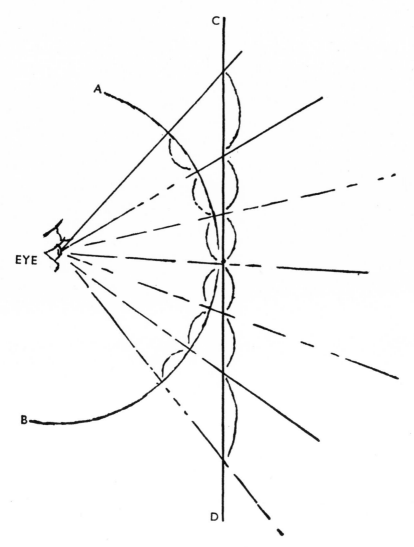

The eye travels over the sphere of vision AB, but projects when drawing onto the flat surface CD. The distortion of scale (and therefore of directions) towards the extremities of vision is indicated

III

As far as systems are concerned, the representational painter should have a grasp of the simple principles of central perspective, because this system approximates closely to our visual sensations and has been widely used since the Renaissance by European painters. He will then recognise its use in other painters, and he will be able to avoid its traps—for there are circumstances in which central perspective, like any other system, breaks down and becomes an obvious distortion. (I suggest that even the painter who eschews the use of 'perspective' should learn its primary rules, or he may find himself using it when he does not mean to.)

Central perspective assumes that the eye selects one point on the horizon (on the viewer's own horizontal level), known as the Centre of Vision. The artificial assumption is that he can also see everything else that concerns him in perfect focus from this point. In fact he is seeing everything else out of the corner of his eye. The system then assumes that all parallel lines in nature converge to common vanishing points. For those parallel lines departing from the eye, which are in nature horizontal, the vanishing point will be on the horizon, for those which slope upwards or downwards it will be above or below the horizon. It also *normally* assumes that all vertical lines remain parallel: though if the eye is so depressed or so elevated in looking at its subject—i.e. looking down into a quarry, looking up at a clock tower—then this is clearly nonsensical. In such cases the eye selects an artificial horizon below or above the true horizon. Parallel lines which are 'flat-on' to the eye remain parallel. As to intervals in depth—think of the time-honoured telegraph poles and railway sleepers of perspective diagrams—the eye must measure one interval in depth and transfer it to paper; the rest follow mechanically. Assume a chessboard landscape. A horizontal line (parallel to the horizon) can be divided into equal parts. It is necessary to measure *one* distance backwards relative to these horizontal parts in order to find the next horizontal line. Now the departing sides will all, according to the rules, meet on the horizon in a 'vanishing point'. You will see that it then becomes possible to draw a diagonal which will cut the horizon at another vanishing point. Because in nature all the diagonals are parallel to each other they will also converge on this vanishing point, and they will intersect the departing sides at diminishing intervals. If you try to produce this system too far into the foreground it becomes evidently a distortion of a real chessboard view; you should try this out to prove it to yourself.

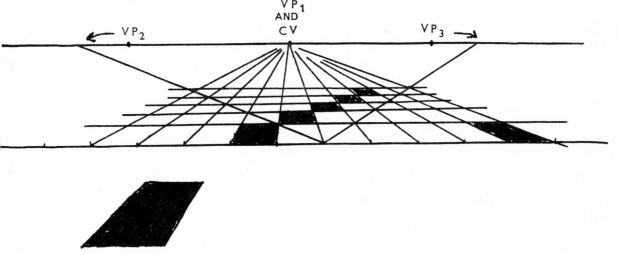

A chequer board surface in central perspective. Centre of vision and vanishing points are shown. The foreground rectangle shows the distortion of a square projected too near the viewer's stand-point

In central perspective circles seen obliquely become ellipses, as in nature. The shape of the ellipse is best found by drawing in perspective the square which surrounds the circle in nature. There is one slightly difficult rule about ellipses which it is worth mastering. Ellipses have longer and shorter axes. If an ellipse represents something (a wheel, arch, clockface) at eye level, that is with its centre on the horizon, then the long axis is vertical. If, however, the ellipse is either above or below your eye level, this is no longer so. The easiest way to determine how it should 'go' is to draw, *in perspective towards its vanishing point,* an imaginary 'spindle' through the centre of your proposed ellipse. The long axis of the ellipse will then be at right angles to this *on your flat drawing surface:* this right angle is *not* in perspective. Failure to observe this rule makes arches, etc., look as though they are falling outwards (*see page 83*).

113

These are the very briefest rules of perspective and I think they are enough for the purpose of this book. There are many elaborations, but they all lead from first principles. A painter is more likely to be able to manipulate perspective for his own purposes if he acquires the habit of working out what he needs from these first principles. There are text-books readily to be found which will lead you further into the subject—but my advice is to play about with the simple rules first until you are familiar with them. The books will show you that other systems of perspective have been invented for special purposes: 'isometric' perspective, for instance, in which parallel lines remain parallel instead of 'vanishing', has particular diagrammatic uses; you will find a form of it in Japanese prints.

But do not be bullied by perspective systems. They exist to help you control depth and scale, but they must not be allowed to override your artistic intentions; if ever rules were made to be broken they are those of perspective.

VI Squaring up accurately

1 Decide where your 'frame' is to fit round your drawing. If your canvas size is predetermined, as in diagram 3 (30″ × 25″) you must adjust the measurements round your drawing to this proportion. The drawing may of course occupy a larger or smaller rectangle than the one I have shown.

2 Rule the centre lines of your picture accurately.

3 Tick off *from the centre outwards* the marks for your squares. Repeat these along two sides, also from the centre. Choose a convenient 'round figure' for these squares, $\frac{1}{4}″$, $\frac{1}{2}″$, 1 centimetre, depending on the size of the drawing. It is *not* necessary by this method for the rectangle to divide into an exact number of squares. The outermost rows of squares will overlap or fall short of the boundary. Do *not* square up blank areas of the drawing where there is no information.

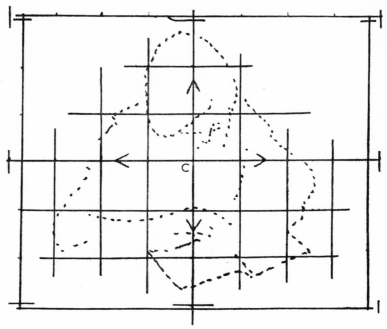

4 A little arithmetic. How big must the squares on your canvas be?

if (x)= the squares on your canvas
    0·5= the squares on your drawing
    30"= the longer side of your canvas
    4·2= the longer side of your drawing

then
$$\frac{x}{0\cdot5}=\frac{30}{4\cdot2} \quad \text{or} \quad x=\frac{30\times0\cdot5}{4\cdot2}$$
$$=3\cdot5''$$

(If you want to be *very* accurate= 3·51")

5 Find the *longer* centre line of your canvas. Bisect it. You now have the centre of your canvas (A). *Do not* mark off the other centre line from the sides of the canvas, but rule it off at right angles from centre (A). This is because stretched canvases are not always as rectangular as they should be.

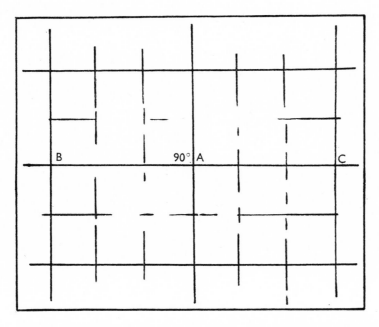

6 The next stage sounds tiresome, but makes all the difference between accuracy and error. Take a rule which if possible extends across your canvas
(in this case a 3-foot rule) and mark on it with a pencil the *cumulative* positions
of your squares, i.e. 3·5″, 7″, 10·5″, 14″, 17·5″ etc. Mark these off on your
centre lines—the rule should not be moved while you are doing this. Draw
right angles through B and C and repeat the process of marking off. The
final squaring up is apparent from diagram 6.

N.B.—If you mark off the squares on your canvas by continually moving a
short ruler 3·5″ along, you will almost certainly accumulate errors,
and they will be different errors on different lines. You should also
avoid this, of course, when squaring up your drawing. Shaky squaring
up usually arises from this, and from relying on the sides of the canvas
as a basis of measurement.

7 At this stage you may find you want greater 'coverage' of your drawing

than the squares provide. This can be quadrupled by ruling the diagonals on drawing and canvas.

8 Number off your grid (with charcoal on the canvas) to identify the squares.

For ruling lines on the canvas you can use charcoal as long as you keep to a sharp point. Pencil strikes through paint disconcertingly. I prefer a fine brush, and use turpentine stained with terre verte.

A final word

This book is an introduction to the technique of oil painting. I have done no more than show some possible ways of setting about this very difficult pursuit; starting points which may help you to enlarge your experience in other and perhaps new directions. I have tried, up to a point, to be objective, but no painter can help but have his prejudices and preferences; no doubt I display them myself. However, I am inclined to think that the completely all-round, impartial and impassive view of painting does not often provide either the best criticism or the most useful practical advice. Many revealing words have been written by good painters in the course of revealing their own allegiances, and they may well help you to a better understanding of painting. If Roger Fry championed Cézanne somewhat at the expense of other fine artists, yet he had many good things to say about Cézanne. Sickert wrote patronizingly of Cézanne, but yet was a wonderfully acute admirer of other Impressionists. And again, you will not find much in praise of Expressionism in the works of André Lhôte, that stern partisan of the Cubist intellect; yet no one has written more passionately on behalf of the classical intelligence in painting.

In other words, when you seek advice or teaching, do not expect that somewhere you will find the last authoritative word on the subject. We may agree that banal and commonplace painting is bad painting, and clearly teaching which leads a good talent along this path is also bad. But there is no completely right way of teaching. The best you can make of it is to sift good advice for your own purposes, and the best of this advice will come from painters with convictions of their own.

Some reliable artists' colourmen and suppliers

In the United Kingdom

Lechertier Barbe Ltd, 95 Jermyn Street, London SW1

Reeves and Sons Ltd, Lincoln Road, Enfield, Middlesex

Robersons and Co Ltd, 71 Parkway, London NW1

George Rowney and Co Ltd, 10 Percy Street, London W1

Winsor and Newton Ltd, 51 Rathbone Place, London W1

In the United States

Grumbacher, 460 West 34th Street, New York, N.Y.
    'Hyplar' (plastic colours) and other materials

New Masters Art Division: California Products Corporation, 169 Waverley Street, Cambridge, Massachusetts
    Produce a new form of tubed plastic paint

Permanent Pigments, Cincinnati, Ohio
    'Liquitex' (acrylic colours) in jars and tubes, and other materials

Shiva, Paducah, Kentucky
    Plastic colours in tubes, and other materials

Weber and Co, New York, N.Y.
    Materials of many kinds

The Author and Publishers would like to thank all those by whose kind permission the following pages of illustrations have been reproduced. Unless otherwise stated, thanks are due to the Royal College of Art for permission to reproduce the work done by artists when they were students there.

1 *'St Peter's denial of Christ': a mosaic from the Basilica of S. Appollinare Nuovo*
Reproduced by courtesy of the University of Bologna

2 'Self-portrait': Rembrandt

3 'Le Pont de Courbevoie':
Georges Seurat

*Reproduced by courtesy of the Trustees of
the Courtauld Institute Galleries, London*

4 'Le Pont de Maincy': Cézanne
Reproduced by courtesy of The Louvre, Paris

5 'Café des Tribunaux, Dieppe':
W. R. Sickert
Reproduced by courtesy of the Trustees of
the Tate Gallery, London

6 '*Notre Dame*': *Henri Matisse*
Reproduced by courtesy of the Trustees of the Tate Gallery, London and Spadem 1965

7 *Sonia Lawson*
'*The Raising of Lazarus*': *an imaginative subject.
The information assembled from studies of models
is cleverly transposed to suit the formality of the
idea. Notice how the drawing accents play a part
in the painting, and help to emphasise tonal
changes. They are not used merely to reinforce an
inadequate design. The design of this work is in
fact most effective*

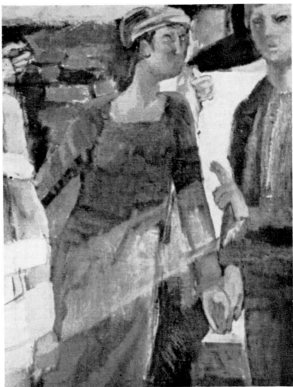

8 *Edward Hamlyn*
This self-portrait has a very robust energetic texture. But the brush strokes nevertheless are directed by the form, and are not plastered in irrationally. There is much care in the drawing behind the apparent immediacy

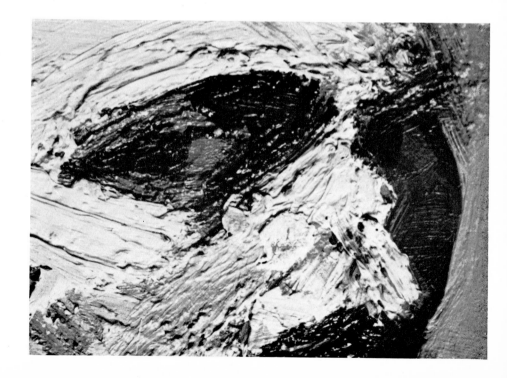

9 *Anthony Messenger*
In this nude the rough blocks of paint suggest an analogy with landscape. This would not succeed if the drawing were literal and over-emphasised the feminine element. It works because the drawing arises out of the conception: the paint and the shapes are consistent

10 *Nevele Tipper*

*Compare this with 13 where the repose of
the subject is emphasised with flat areas of
paint. Here the 'action' of a similar subject
is brought out by the strong movement of the
brush marks across the planes. The 'build-
up' to white from black is clearly seen*

11 *Brian Hagger*

The rich impasto used here is appropriate to the subject-matter. The contrasts in surface between sky, building and road prevent the picture becoming 'imprisoned' behind its texture (always a danger with such assertively heavy paint)

12 *Brian Hagger*
As in 11 the subtle variety of texture allows the thick impasto to give a simple unity to the picture surface without becoming more important than the subject it describes. The paint marks say something true without being imitative

13 *Irena Delderfield*

You need not look beyond everyday situations for pictorial drama which is suggested here by the contrast of breadth and detail. A few simple tones supply all the depth necessary, and they are placed on the hardboard panel with a minimum of modelling. The 'abstract' shown leaning against the wall becomes part of the picture

14 *Keith Lucas*

The paint surface is reserved and even. It allows for a maximum contrast of character in the different shapes of things, which might be defeated by a dominating texture

15 *Elizabeth Keys*
In this portrait the carefully resolved character of each shape allows the paint to remain simple and expressive

16 *Michael Hoar*

In this studio interior the subject is very much about the light, and its invasion of all the surfaces. Form is hinted at by tone and perspective. The paint surface is appropriately thin and swift; a heavy impasto might concentrate the attention too much on individual objects

17 *Brian Ingham*
This acutely observed analysis of detailed textures allows no half measures. Where the paint must by nature of the detail be thin, there is no help from bravura brush work. The control must come, as it does here, from a firmly maintained tonal pattern

18 *Harold Parkin*

'Idyllic' subjects are very difficult to bring off as well as this. The slight naïveté disguises a very careful design. The paint is quiet and unassertive, not interfering with the 'narrative' quality. But above all this painting avoids the archness and facetiousness which are fatal to so many attempts at this kind of subject

19 *Andrew McLaren*
This design is splendidly contained by the diagonal sweep of figures. The contrary action of the leg of the top figure on the right stabilises the movement, and the whole group is thrust into prominence by the dark landscape

20 *John Ridgewell*

A semi-imaginary landscape built from a number of experiences. In such a case it is appropriate that the paint surface should assert itself as a decorative and unifying element. In more actual or literal subject-matter it might become aggressive; here it is an integral part of the idea

21 *Frederick Cuming*

This landscape shows how the brush can summarise the varied character of a whole group of trees, and this is carried out mostly along its silhouette. There is a minimum of interference between lights and dark, so that where a white accent is used, as in the white shirt sleeve, it has the greatest effect

22 *Patricia Sullivan*
This rather formalised nude shows how blocks and strokes of colour simplifying the surfaces can be built up to a satisfying whole without any imitative detail

23 *Kenneth Beresford*
A very every-day subject in which a formal idea has been searched out without loss of authenticity

24 *Andrew McLaren*

*The clear technical treatment of this work
has been used to overcome what might be an
unmanageable complexity of subject-matter.
The accents of dark lines for the furniture
and a few selected highlights are set off
against (and on top of) a broad series of
tonal masses, simply swept into with thin
paint. This is 'technique' used in its proper
sense, to resolve a problem*

25 *Charles Hardaker*
The arms of fellow students outstretched in measurement often get in the way. The point of this painting is that their presence, not their absence, was noticed. The point of many paintings is lost because we close our minds to what our eyes can see

26 *Brian Roxby*

The palette knife has been used effectively in the sky where it provides a textural contrast with the more softly painted sea and the dabbed paint of the fore-shore. Again four or five simple tones control the surface

27   *Christopher Clairmonte*
*Painting with linear accents is sometimes a way of
avoiding the real problems, but here the technique
is justifiably used to emphasise the architectural
verticality of the subject*

28 *James Heward*
*The accumulation of tonal marks here repre-
sent the kind of development of a tonal
painting which I suggest in the text. The
form is explained but remains part of the
'pattern' of the design. An example, by the
way, of a grand formal design growing out
of a natural informal pose*

29 *William Cowper*

Painting is here seen in a very 'graphic' mood, the colour being built up very much within the framework of a linear drawing. The painter rightly avoids shadow masses (which are cut to the minimum) and employs the technical approach at its most suitable, in a full-light

30 *Alfred Daniels*

In an imaginative subject piece like this a consistent style of shapes is maintained. Notice how the interest is carried through to the unexpected glimpses of the women's feet and the packages in the window

31 *A portrait by the same artist. The consistent formalising does preclude the closest observation, as in the drawing of the hands*

32 *Jacqueline Stanley*

In a portrait it is only too easy to become over-imitative. Here everything has been said with direct brushmarks laid side by side and superimposed, dark to light. The paint has not been 'fussed about' or fused together for the sake of smoothness

33 *William Cowper*

A still-life by the painter of 29. Again, a very calligraphic approach to the subject. Directness of statement is an essential quality in such a method

34 *Beryl Lewis*

The particular merit of the 'technique' in this painting is that it allows the artist to move from breadth to detail with no inconsistency. In general the less limiting the technique the better it is. Here the paint is put on unselfconsciously; it is very well done, but we are asked to look at the subject not at a display of virtuosity

35 *St Francis' Church, Clifton Estate, Nottingham*

Pamela Lloyd

A study from a church ceiling. In position, the painting shows how the diminution in scale of the figures helps to enhance the length of the ceiling

36 *Keith Grant   A mural painting in progress. The whole work was squared up from very careful drawings. The design is kept nearly flat in order to preserve the feeling of the wall surface*

Below: A part of the same mural completed and in position

37 *Albert Herbert*
A life study in black crayon which combines most of the draughtsman's resources. Silhouette, contour, line, cast, shadow and local colour all play their part. Notice how much variety has gone into explaining the crossing of the wrist over the further thigh

38 *Julia Levine*
A drawing which is very much a silhouette. The hints of light on the figure turn the white paper into a source of illumination

39 *Jonathan McClenning*
A drawing whose technical mean is the local colour of the figure. The subtle hints of light show that the source of light is in front. The overlapping of the sheet in front of the arm does a great deal to establish the surface on which the figure is lying

40 *Beryl Lewis*

*Three studies in soft pencil. The open line and the
tone are developed together to give a sense of light.
In the drawing of the seated man the local colour of
the dark suit has been used positively. All these are
drawings which could lead straight into paintings*

41 *Nevele Tipper*

*A charcoal study for a landscape painting. A great deal of
the subtle variety of lines that could be exploited in paint is
already worked out here*

Index

163